The Jail

THE JAIL

MANAGING THE UNDERCLASS IN AMERICAN SOCIETY

John Irwin

UNIVERSITY OF CALIFORNIA PRESS

Berkeley   Los Angeles   London

University of California Press
Berkeley and Los Angeles, California

University of California Press, Ltd.
London, England

Library of Congress Cataloging in Publication Data

Irwin, John, 1929–
    The jail: managing the underclass in American society.

    Bibliography: p.
    Includes index.
    1. Jails—Social aspects—California—Case
    studies. 2. Prisoners—California—Case studies.
    3. Prison psychology.   I. Title.
HV8324.I79   1986   365'.6'0979461   85–1155
ISBN 0–520–05563–2 (alk. paper)

Printed in the United States of America

1   2   3   4   5   6   7   8   9

*To Erving Goffman,
who tried to teach me,
but I wouldn't learn*

Contents

Tables

Preface

Social scientists, like the general public, have shown a great interest in the prison but have almost completely ignored the jail. Since John Howard's historic report on English jails, *The State of the Prisons in England and Wales* (1777), there have been perhaps a dozen other reports (most of which are listed in the bibliography), whereas there are hundreds of studies on the prison. The opposite focus is more appropriate for several reasons. First, many more people pass through the jail. The estimates range from 3 to 7 million a year in the United States, and this is at least thirty times the number handled by all state and federal prisons. Second, when persons are arrested, the most critical decisions about their future freedom are made while they are either in jail or attached to it by a bail bond. These decisions, like the decision to arrest, are often highly discretionary and raise disturbing questions about the whole criminal justice system. Third, the experiences prisoners endure while passing through the jail often drastically influence their lives. Finally, the jail, not the prison, imposes the cruelest form of punishment in the United States.

Although recognizing the jail was more important, I too concentrated on the prison for many years. In the mid-1970s I made one attempt to begin a study of the the jail after Richard Hongisto, a personal friend, was elected sheriff of San Francisco and agreed to give me full access to the three jails he administered—no small matter, because social scientists have had more difficulty approaching the jail than the prison. However, the prison issue continued to absorb me, and I did not take up the offer. Finally, in 1979, after finishing a book on prisons, I again resolved to study the jail. Though Hongisto had resigned and a less adventurous sheriff had been appointed to replace him, Hongisto had created a prisoner services program through which I was able to circulate in the San Francisco jails. Prisoner services attempts to fill jail prisoners' myriad needs: contact with families, lawyers, friends, and employers; removal of detainers from other jurisdictions; and recovery of personal property. (In the middle of my research Michael Hennessey, a former prisoner services lawyer, was elected sheriff of San Francisco and gave full support to my study.) In 1979 and 1980 I was a caseworker on the felony floors of the three San Francisco jails that hold pretrial detainees. Several times a day I visited the felony "tanks" (large cells holding a number of prisoners) to gather "requests for action," clarify the requests that had been forwarded to the prisoner services' offices, and tell prisoners the response to their requests. On these visits I soon moved from outside the tank to inside where I engaged in many informal conversations with prisoners. Also I interviewed selected prisoners in private.

After observing in the jail for a year, I left prisoner services and for several months accompanied public defenders to their various hearings. During this period I also interviewed and accompanied persons working for the San Francisco OR project, a program for the release of prisoners on their own recognizance.

By spring 1981 I had formed a particularly significant impression: the vast majority of prisoners in the jail were very different from the popular conception of a criminal. I needed to strengthen this impression with firmer data, so I randomly selected 100 persons charged with felonies and 100 charged with misdemeanors from the booking records at the jail. With Nancy Strachan, a research assistant, I interviewed the felony arrestees and followed both samples' cases through the jail and the court records until they were resolved. (A more complete description of this phase of the study appears at the beginning of Chapter 2.)

Although I studied the San Francisco jails, my findings may be relevant to jails in general. During my work I was a part of a broader study of three county jails—San Francisco, Yolo, and Los Angeles. I not only consulted the quantitative data gathered in these studies, but I made several visits to the Yolo County jails and the main county jail in Los Angeles. Moreover, having been a prisoner in eight different city and county jails for periods up to 120 days, I have firsthand experience with jails. Finally, I have drawn from the literature on jails to verify, compare, and correct my own findings.

I selected San Francisco's jails because of their availability, but they were also appropriate to the study. The San Francisco County jails represent a type of jail, the "big-city" jail. San Francisco is near the median in age, decrepitude, range of facilities, level of deprivation, and overall harshness imposed on prisoners. Its only uniqueness derives from ten years of very active reform-minded sheriffs since 1972 and the differences they effectuated. Moreover, there are powerful contextual forces that produce similarities in jails, particularly in big-city jails.

I ignored women in jail primarily because I based most of the study on my own participation, spending much time at the tanks and other locations in the men's jail. I did not feel that it would be appropriate to attempt to do this in the women's jail. (I also doubt that I would have been allowed to.) Besides, women are a notably different jail population and require a separate study.

Most of my attention was on pretrial prisoners and the pretrial processes. Though they constitute only about half of the prisoners, pretrial detainees are in many respects the more significant ones. Historically, jails have been mainly places to hold persons for trial. The sentencing function was added relatively recently and more as an adjacent development to the penitentiaries, the first major prisons used in the United States for punishment. The pretrial phase remains the most controversial (because of the judicial theory of innocence until conviction), most relevant to the judicial processes, and most consequential to prisoners. Therefore, I give much less attention to the sentencing phase.

My critical discovery was that instead of "criminals," the jail receives and confines mostly detached and disreputable persons who are arrested more because they are offensive than because they have committed crimes. Moreover, I learned that the primary purpose of the jail is to manage these persons, whom I finally decided to call the *rabble*. I also discovered that in managing the rabble by arresting them and holding them in jail, society inadvertently increases their number and holds people in a rabble status.

These ideas are the focus of the book. Chapter 1 examines the purpose of the jail as rabble management by presenting a brief history of the jail in England and America. Chapter 2 shows who goes to jail and what they go there for. Chapters 3, 4, 5, and 6 describe in detail what actually happens to people who are arrested and jailed and explores some of the frequent personal and social consequences of that experience. In Chapter 7, I discuss in broad sociological terms the problems related to reforming the jail.

Acknowledgments

Several persons attached to the San Francisco Sheriff's Department made it possible for me to study the San Francisco jails. Former Sheriff Richard Hongisto had created prisoner services, through which I was admitted into the jail. Guy Crouch, who was the director of prisoner services when I began my research, actually accepted me into prisoner services, which gained my clearance at the jail. Many other prisoner services staff—particularly Lou Valla, Ron Perez, Ann Walls, Mike Marcum, Andrea Elukovich, David Hoerl, Johnnie Drennon, Willy Gray, and Richard Baxter—assisted me in my work. Michael Hennessey was elected sheriff in the middle of the study and gave me full cooperation. Several people in the San Francisco OR project and the public defender's office, particularly Ken Babb, Wendy Mengel, Peter Keane, Marla Zamora, and Mogel Christanson, also helped me considerably.

Nancy Strachan assisted me with some of the research and the analysis of data. Louise Doyle also assisted in this phase of the research.

In the spring of 1981 I received a grant from the National Institute of Corrections (NIC), which allowed me to complete the second half of a year's leave from teaching, during which I began writing this book. I must thank Allen Breed, who was the director of NIC at that time and made this grant possible. Also, Bruce Bounds at NIC's Jail Center was helpful during the period of the grant and especially during a visit I made to the center. Paul Katsampes and Mark Pogerebin, also

at the center, read chapters, made suggestions, and arranged two for-
ums at which I presented ideas from my work.

During 1983 I was attached to a study of the jail conducted by the
National Council of Crime and Delinquency funded by the National
Institute of Justice. James Austin and Pat Jackson, who conducted that
study, provided me access to the Los Angeles and Yolo County jails,
supplied me with data, and reviewed drafts of my study.

I experienced many difficulties in organizing and writing this book
and am indebted to a very large number of people who assisted me
along the way. My wife, Marsha Rosenbaum, read each draft and made
thoughtful comments. Sheldon Messinger, Troy Duster, David Well-
man, Barbara Owen, James Austin, and D. Alan Henry read whole or
parts of drafts and made constructive comments. David Matza, David
Minkus, and Hardy Frey discussed the study with me and made valu-
able suggestions. Carol Warren and Howard Becker read it more than
once and assisted me tremendously. The comments of U.C. Press's
anonymous reviewers were very helpful; one person in particular gave
the manuscript three thorough readings.

Finally, I wish to acknowledge the in-depth contribution of Gene
Tanke, who edited the final draft and is largely responsible for its
readability.

1

Managing Rabble

I N   A   LEGAL   SENSE, the jail is the point of entry into the criminal justice system. It is the place where arrested persons are booked and where they are held for their court appearances if they cannot arrange bail. It is also the city or county detention facility for persons serving misdemeanor sentences, which in most states cannot exceed one year. The prison, on the other hand, is a state or federal institution that holds persons serving felony sentences, which generally run to more than one year.

The public impression is that the jail holds a collection of dangerous criminals. But familiarity and close inspection reveal that the jail holds only a very few persons who fit the popular conception of a criminal— a predator who seriously threatens the lives and property of ordinary citizens. In fact, the great majority of the persons arrested and held in jail belong to a different social category. Some students of the jail have politely referred to them as the poor: "American jails operate primarily as catchall asylums for poor people."[1] Some have added other correlates of poverty: "With few exceptions, the prisoners are poor, undereducated, unemployed, and they belong to minority groups."[2] Some use more imaginative and sociologically suggestive labels, such as "social refuse" or "social junk."[3] Political radicals sometimes use "lumpen proletariat" and argue over whether its members are capable of participating in the class struggle.[4] Some citizens refer to persons in

1

this category as "street people," implying an excessive and improper public presence. Others apply such labels as "riffraff," "social trash," or "dregs," which suggest lack of social worth and moral depravity. And many police officers, deputies, and other persons who are familiar with the jail population use more crudely derogatory labels, such as "assholes" and "dirt balls."

In my own research, I found that beyond poverty and its corre-lates—undereducation, unemployment, and minority status—jail prisoners share two essential characteristics: detachment and disre-pute. They are detached because they are not well integrated into con-ventional society, they are not members of conventional social orga-nizations, they have few ties to conventional social networks, and they are carriers of unconventional values and beliefs. They are disreputa-ble because they are perceived as irksome, offensive, threatening, ca-pable of arousal, even protorevolutionary. In this book I shall refer to them as the *rabble*, meaning the "disorganized" and "disorderly," the "lowest class of people."[5]

I found that it is these two features—detachment and disrepute—that lead the police to watch and arrest the rabble so frequently, regard-less of whether or not they are engaged in crime, or at least in serious crime. (Most of the rabble commit petty crimes, such as drinking on the street, and are usually vulnerable to arrest.)

These findings suggest that the basic purpose of the jail differs rad-ically from the purpose ascribed to it by government officials and aca-demicians. It is this: the jail was invented, and continues to be oper-ated, in order to manage society's rabble. Society's impulse to manage the rabble has many sources, but the subjectively perceived "offen-siveness" of the rabble is at least as important as any real threat it poses to society.

The contemporary jail is a subsidiary to the welfare organizations that are intended to "regulate the poor." Frances Fox Piven and Rich-ard Cloward have pointed out that when masses of occupationally dis-located people pose a threat, society applies social control devices, such as relief programs:

> When large numbers of people are suddenly barred from their tradi-tional occupations, the entire structure of social control is weakened and may even collapse. There is no harvest or paycheck to enforce work and the sentiments that uphold work; without work, people cannot con-form to familial and communal roles; and if the dislocation is wide-spread, the legitimacy of the social order itself may come to be ques-

tioned. The result is usually civil disorder—crime, mass protests, riots— a disorder that may even threaten to overturn existing social and economic arrangements. It is then that relief programs are initiated or expanded.[6]

However, from among the poor there will also emerge a rabble who are perceived as a more serious and constant threat to the social order, a group in need of the more direct forms of social control delivered by the criminal justice system. Usually the more violent and rapacious rabble are arrested, convicted, and sent to prison; the merely offensive are held in jail. The jail was devised as, and continues to be, the special social device for controlling offensive rabble. To demonstrate this proposition, I will review briefly the history of the jail in England and its later development in America.

Historical Development of the English Jail

All ancient cities used some method of detaining persons in order to impose punishment. According to Hans Mattick: "Unscalable pits, dungeons, suspended cages, and sturdy trees to which prisoners were chained pending trial are some of the predecessors of the jail."[7] As early as the ninth century in England, Alfred the Great's laws mentioned imprisonment: "If he, however, pledge what is right for him to fulfill, and belie that, let him give with lowly mindedness his weapon and his goods to his friends to hold, and be forty nights in prison in a king's town, and suffer there as the Bishop assigns him; and let his kinsmen feed him if he himself have no meat."[8] Probably the persons sentenced were held in castles or monastery buildings. And in his history of imprisonment in England, Ralph Pugh notes: "There is no doubt that the Normans found a number of prisons in the England that they invaded, particularly upon royal manors in the south, and, in effect, they added to their number. This they did by building many castles in which both king and barons shut up their powerful adversaries and during the Anarchy very many of the common people also."[9]

The jail, however, was a new institution in medieval England. It was a special structure, erected and administered by the local authority, the sheriff, for the sole purpose of holding persons to be delivered to the royal courts for judgment. Sheriffs began establishing jails in the early eleventh century or slightly before.[10] By 1166, Henry II, the powerful Norman king, "enjoined all sheriffs to ensure that in all counties where no gaols existed gaols should now be built."[11]

The need for this new institution arose from a great increase in the number of detached persons. At this time, England, along with all of Europe, was moving out of feudalism with its isolated, mostly autonomous fiefdoms. By the late eleventh century Muslim control of the Mediterranean had ended, and trade once again began to connect European populations and to result in the cultivation of urban centers.[12] New towns appeared, and towns grew into cities. European kings began reestablishing and extending their hegemonies. After having remained stable for centuries, the population in most parts of Europe was increasing. At the same time, the feudal system was unraveling. More and more persons were cut loose from the land and from the two basic social organizations of the agricultural society, the family and the tribe.[13] Henri Pirenne, in tracing the development of the merchant class, describes this well. Speaking of the increase in population, he writes:

> It had as a result the detaching from the land [of] an increasingly important number of individuals and committing them to the roving and hazardous existence which, in every agricultural civilization, is the lot of those who no longer find themselves with their roots in the soil. It multiplied the crowd of vagabonds drifting about all through society, living from day to day by alms from the monasteries, hiring themselves out at harvest-time, enlisting in the armies in time of war and holding back from neither rapine nor pillage when occasion presented.[14]

Some of the newly uprooted found more or less legitimate means to survive within the changing social order. As feudalism gave way to mercantilism, some new jobs appeared. The ongoing wars, and especially the Crusades, occupied (and killed) many; mendicant religious orders absorbed some; and the recurring plagues eliminated many thousands. Nevertheless, a large portion of the displaced became part of the rabble. Outlaws who lived by robbing, plundering, poaching, and smuggling abounded in the forests and countryside. (The legend of Robin Hood comes from these times.) Disreputable persons filled the towns and the cities. As Urban Tigner Holmes reports:

> The *ribauz*, or good-for-nothings, were always on the edge of a crowd. They begged and plundered at the slightest provocation. They hung around outside the door of the banquet hall when a large feast was held. The king of England had three hundred bailiffs whose duty it was— though not all at one time—to keep these people back as food was

moved from the kitchens to the hall, and to see that guests were not disturbed. Frequently in twelfth-century romances a beautiful damsel is threatened with the awful fate of being turned over to the *ribauz*. Nothing more horrible can be imagined. These people accompanied armies on their expeditions, helping in menial tasks and plundering what was left by the knights and other fighting men.[15]

The growth of the rabble had two important influences on the social-control efforts of English rulers. In the first place, it presented them with new social problems to which they responded with increasingly punitive measures, which reached their peak at the end of the eighteenth century with the notorious Grand Assizes and the excessive use of the death penalty.[16] In the second place, it made necessary a drastic increase in the use of imprisonment for detention before trial. Historically, before the number of detached persons grew troublesome, it was considered unnecessary to hold a person before judgment had been passed. With few exceptions, persons were trusted because they were firmly connected to the church, guild, tribe, community, or town; only the occasional unattached person charged with an offense might need some special provision. For example, Alfred the Great, the ninth-century Anglo-Saxon king who stabilized England after the Danish invasions, attempted to ensure the appearance of displaced suspects by attaching them to local citizens:

If such a stranger, merchant, or wayfaring man, came to be suspected of any crime and could not be found, he whose guest he had last been was summoned to account for him. If he had not entertained the stranger for more than two nights, he might clear himself by oath; but if the stranger had lodged with him three nights, he was bound to produce him, or answer, and pay "weregild," or "wite," for him, as for one of his own family.[17]

However, by the end of the eleventh century the number of detached people milling about the countryside and in the towns had given rise to the use of bail or detention in the newly erected jails. Pugh points out that in the beginning bail was more common than detention: "Attachment followed by release on bail was the method that was first adopted by those officers [sheriffs] in securing the arraignment of offenders and it never fell out of use or even grew uncommon. It seems reasonably clear, however, that, as time went on, actual confinement progressively supplemented attachment and bail as the surer means of attaining the needful aim."[18] What occurred "as time went on" was that the number of displaced people charged with crimes continued to increase. This was because not only the numbers of the rabble but also the likelihood of their being charged with a crime greatly increased over the next centuries. The English rulers passed more and more laws designed to control the rabble, to stop their incursions on private property, and, when shortages of labor existed, to assign them to low-paid productive work.The vagrancy laws passed between 1349 and 1743 were intended for these purposes.*

The increasing threat attributed to the rabble may be seen in a later statute that prescribes death for "ruffians" who a second time "shall wander, loiter, or idle use themselves and play vagabond."[19] In the sixteenth century, England introduced the less blatantly cruel and punitive workhouses, called bridewells, to manage and reform the poor.[20] By the middle of the eighteenth century, in many counties the "county gaol [was] also a bridewell"; and many of the prisoners sentenced to houses of correction, to be engaged in hard labor in order to reform them, were actually idle and were treated the same as the felons and debtors held in the jails.[21] By the nineteenth century, the bridewells, as well as the poorhouses, had been completely amalgamated with the jails.[22]

English colonists brought the tradition of the jail with them to America, but in their first half-century in the New World they did not rely on it very heavily.[23] The early settlers were mostly respectable people—middle class and religious—and the few rabble among them were manageable by expulsion, which was feasible in North America with its vast areas between towns and cities and its open frontier. The few nonrabble offenders were released on bail until adjudication and then fined, publicly shamed, whipped, banished, or, in a few cases,

---

*Caleb Foote, who studied the abuses of vagrancy statutes, interprets these laws:

The anti-migratory policy behind vagrancy legislation began as an essential complement of the wage stabilization legislation which accompanied the breakup of feudalism and the depopulation caused by the Black Death. By the Statutes of Labourers in 1349-1351, every able-bodied person without other means of support was required to work for wages fixed at the level preceding the Black Death; it was unlawful to accept more, or to refuse an offer to work, or to flee from one county to another to avoid offers of work or to seek higher wages, or to give alms to able-bodied beggars who refused to work. (Foote, "Vagrancy Type Law and Its Administration," p. 615)

executed. Incarceration was not used.[24] During the eighteenth century, however, members of other social classes, including thousands of transported disreputables, many of them convicts, poured in. Many towns and all cities constructed jails. Still, the threat of the rabble was not as great as it was in England, and so these early jails were small and much more humanely managed than England's. They were patterned after rooming houses, and the prisoners suffered no restrictions other than the confinement.[25]

At the end of the eighteenth century the problem of managing the growing urban rabble increased, and several eastern cities—notably Philadelphia, New York, and Boston—constructed larger jails, such as Newgate in New York and the Walnut Street jail in Philadelphia. The disreputability and the increased number of prisoners are suggested in the following description of the Walnut Street jail shortly after the Revolutionary War:

> It is represented as a scene of promiscuous and unrestricted intercourse, and universal riot and debauchery. There was no separation of color, age or sex, by day or by night; the prisoners lying promiscuously on the floor, most of them without anything like bed or bedding. As soon as the sexes were placed in different wings, which was the first reform made in the prison, of thirty or forty women then confined there, all but four or five immediately left it; it having been a common practice, it is said, for women to cause themselves to be arrested for fictitious debts, that they might share in the orgies of the place. Intoxicating liquours abounded, and indeed were freely sold at a bar kept by one of the officers of the prison.[26]

After the war Americans began building huge "asylums" to remove, manage, punish, and reform problem populations (most of them the rabble). All cities also built large county and city jails. Although these new jails were smaller versions of the fortresslike asylums (particularly the penitentiaries), no humanitarian theory of reform, no justification through public debate, in fact no plan at all accompanied their development. They were merely "super-secure, fenced, ugly, uncomfortable and unsafe, totally deprived environments."[27] This architectural program has been followed, with a few exceptions, up to the present day.

Later in the nineteenth century, when the smaller towns in the West and Midwest began to be bothered by the detached, transient, and disreputable rabble—mostly drunken miners, trappers, cowboys, and "outlaws"—small jails appeared. The first, which was typical of the type, was "a building of cottonwood two by fours built in the early 1870s. In its narrow confines of six by eighteen feet as many as forty law breakers were kept at one time, largely cowboys who had shown too much exuberance upon reaching town."[28]

After the Civil War, as more predatory and violent rabble appeared in the Midwest and West—notably the various bank-robbing and train-robbing gangs that descended from Quantrill's Guerrillas (a renegade band that operated during and after the Civil War), such as the James brothers, the Youngers, and the Starrs—some towns experimented with more elaborate and secure jails. One example was the "rotary" jail, which had a permanent steel-barred cylinder with an opening on each floor. On the inside of this was another revolving steel-barred cylinder that was divided into pie-shaped cells, each of which had a door opening. Exit was possible only as the cell door rotated to the opening on the outside cylinder.[29]

By 1900 Americans had taken England's rabble management invention and modified it to suit their own needs. In particular, in their expanding industrial cities they were ready with large city and county jails to manage the urban rabble, whose numbers and offensiveness were increasing.

Managing the Rabble in the Modern City

Industrialization greatly increased the number of displaced persons, most of whom crowded into the rapidly expanding cities. Fear of the rabble—or "the dangerous classes," as they were called in the last century—increased proportionately. In speaking of Victorian London, Kellow Chesney locates the object of this fear:

> When respectable people spoke of the *dangerous classes*—a phrase enjoying a good deal of currency—they were not talking about the labouring population as a whole, nor the growing industrial proletariat. Neither were they referring to that minority of politically conscious, mostly "superior" radical working men on whom any sustained working-class political movement ultimately depended. They meant certain classes of people whose very manner of living seemed a challenge to ordered society and the tissue of laws, moralities and taboos holding it together.

These "unprincipled," "ruffianly," "degraded" elements seemed ready
to exploit any breakdown in the established order.[30]

In the United States, the dangerous classes in the cities were mostly
recent immigrants, which added to the fear:

> In the poorer quarters of our great cities may be found huddled together
> the Italian bandit and the bloodthirsty Spaniard, the bad man from Sic-
> ily, the Hungarian, the Croatian and the Pole, the Chinaman and the
> Negro, the cockney Englishman, the Russian and the Jew, with all the
> centuries of hereditary hate back of them. They continually cross each
> others' path. It is no wonder that altercations occur and blood is shed.[31]

Though they vary with time and place, there is great continuity in
the social types that constitute "the dangerous classes." For example,
Victorian London had its beggars, "gonophs" (petty thieves), bur-
glars, pickpockets, prostitutes, fences, and gamblers and its waves of
itinerant poor that were similar to America's hobos.[32] At a comparable
time in its development, around 1900, New York City had all these
types as well as its own feared "gangs"—such as the Dead Rabbits,
the Bowery Boys, the Eastmans, the Gophers, and the Five Pointers—
who stole, fought, and generally terrorized people in and around the
Five Points and Hell's Kitchen districts of lower Manhattan.[33] Urban
alcoholic derelicts became a part of the American rabble class after the
Civil War. Junkies appeared after the passage of the Harrison Act in
1914 and the shift of opiate addiction to the lower classes.[34] Bootleg-
gers and numbers workers were added in eastern cities in the 1920s.
Though their styles change from year to year, delinquent gangs of male
youths—such as the recent California "lowriders" and the Los Angeles "cholos"—have long been a permanent part of the American urban
class.[35] America today has a sizable detached and deviant population
whose members accumulate in the cities, where their presence in public places offends and threatens conventional people.

The straightforward and punitive measures used in England in the
late Middle Ages to control the growing rabble class—such as the statutes that explicitly outlawed rabble status—can no longer be employed. In the mid-nineteenth century, England itself recoiled from the
excessively punitive methods used against the lower classes and
adopted, in theory at least, a more humanitarian system of penology,
which prohibited this type of direct legislation against the rabble. In
the United States, the rhetoric of equality and basic human rights has

blocked any direct legal approach to controlling the rabble. However, a variety of indirect legal methods have been applied. The "criminalization" of drug and alcohol use was intended to control classes of people as much as to punish deviant behavior of individuals.[36] The state and local vagrancy statutes have also been thinly disguised legal assaults against the rabble status.[37]

Presently, the main systems of control are social segregration and the "peace-keeping" or "watchman" style of police work, which involves the selective use of arrest as well as other discretionary actions, such as verbal commands, threats of arrest, and giving help.[38] As Lyn Lofland has pointed out, the strategy of segregation is part of a general development in the industrial city, which itself has a "segregating tendency": "In many respects, the ideal of the modern city is like the ideal of a well-ordered home: a place for everything and everything in its place."[39] The place for the rabble is in "deviant ghettos," which Paul Rock compares with the medieval English poor sanctuaries established under the Acts of Settlement:

> These acts were designed to enforce immobility upon the poor. People were barred from travel, work, or alien residence. As a kind of shadow parish, sanctuaries and bastard sanctuaries housed the criminal, the debtor, the bankrupt, the pauper, and the eccentric in relatively unpoliced and autonomous areas of geographical and social space. [So, too, in the present] a growing resort to zoning regulation, defensive alliances among residents, the tendency to provide welfare and other provisions in centralized locations, and the economics of housing have worked together to create new sanctuaries. In effect there has been a limited restoration of neo-feudal styles of control. It is unlikely that the new deviant ghettos will be rigorously patrolled unless their populations swamp out over their borders.[40]

On this last point, I take issue. The deviant ghettos are rigorously patrolled. And the primary purpose of this activity is not to enforce the law but rather to keep the peace—which largely means managing the rabble.

Studies of police peace-keeping activities have identified many techniques other than arrest that police officers use to control the rabble both in and out of deviant ghettos.[41] But here we are concerned only with methods that involve arrest.

Containment

Police officers attempt to contain rabble behavior by restricting offensive social types to special neighborhoods and by limiting their deviant activities. The neighborhoods are mainly skid rows, ethnic ghettos, and areas such as San Francisco's Tenderloin and Manhattan's Times Square, which contain a great number of disreputable types and the businesses that cater to them, such as bars, cheap hotels, cheap theaters, sex shows, and massage parlors. In a sense, these zones are given over to the rabble, not because it is recognized that the rabble must have a place, but because there is nothing else that can be done with them. In these zones the police have a mandate to reduce the public deviance to an acceptable level, prevent disreputables from preying excessively on one another, and protect reputable persons who pass through or have business there. As one officer said: "We have girls going to work at the Telephone Company here. They have to walk through this area. We have to provide them with an area they *can* walk through."[42]

Police officers will arrest disreputables in these zones for acting in ways that exceed the police officers' conception of the zone's behavioral limits. This conception is based on unstated, unwritten discretionary standards, which are part of the police officers' working culture and are learned mostly on the job.* Many violations of these discretionary standards are, at most, very petty crimes, and sometimes they consist of nothing more than disobeying an officer's commands or in some other way challenging his authority—and in these zones maintaining authority is an important issue with police. In this study my research assistant and I randomly selected 100 persons arrested for felonies in San Francisco and then interviewed them and reviewed their booking and court records. In twenty-five cases, the persons were engaged in very petty crimes (or no crime at all), but they behaved in ways that apparently exceeded the standards of the rabble zone. Here are a few examples of such behavior, taken from the interviews or from the booking reports of the arresting officer.

A young black male got into a fight with his sister in their home in

---

*Though the limits vary from time to time and officer to officer, in a particular period officers tend to agree on them. For a discussion of the working knowledge of police officers, see Egon Bittner, "The Police on Skid-Row: A Study of Peace Keeping."

one of the city's ethnic ghettos. She called the police and told them that he had hit her with a stick. He claimed that he had not: "I have witnesses that say I didn't touch her." The police believed her version and arrested him.

A young white male described his arrest to me: "I was standing outside a door and the landlady called the police. I was bleeding. I had just been beat up. When they came, they searched me and found some pills. They were nice to me. Took me to get some stitches and then brought me to jail."

In another example, the arresting officers described the arrest in their booking report:

> While on patrol in the area [an ethnic ghetto] I observed E. to be walking from corner to corner with no apparent business. As I observed him further to walk [north bound] on Octavia from Hayes, I entered the radio car, at which time E. took a cigarette package out of his pocket, and threw it onto the stairs of [street number] Octavia, at which time two tablets fell out of the package. Further look at the package produced 24 more white tablets, possibly codeine No. 4. E. was taken into custody and booked.

In trying to keep the zone's public deviant behavior within tolerable limits, police officers watch particular persons and particular types, such as petty hustlers. Three of the arrests in the felony sample were of persons that the police officers knew and defined as potential troublemakers. One of them said: "I was walking down the street through the Tenderloin with some friends. A cop pulls up and says, 'you're drunk.' He grabbed me and we scuffled. I fell down. The cop accused me of trying to steal his gun. It was a set-up. They did the same thing to me a year ago. They're just trying to get my probation revoked."

Six arrests were of petty hustlers who sold drugs in San Francisco's Tenderloin or the South of Market skid row. One member of this group said in an interview: "I was walking down Market Street talking to a friend. Two undercover cops thought I was talking to them [instead of his friend], trying to sell them some weed. They arrested me for possession for sale. It wasn't weed; it was tobacco and herbs."

Two arrests were of Cubans, a group the police see as troublemakers and criminals. In an interview, one Cuban explained (in Spanish) that he had been standing with a friend on the corner of Twentieth and Mission (in the heart of the Latino neighborhood) when the police pulled up to them. He said he did not know what they said because he cannot speak English. They arrested him and his friend for felony assault. (Two days later the charges were dismissed.)

In the rabble zones disreputables often prey on other disreputables, and police officers make arrests to protect the disreputable victims. This apparently was the case in eight of the arrests in our sample. As one man said in his interview: "Me and my ole lady were having an argument on the street. We had been drinking and walking around [in the Tenderloin]. She stepped out in the street and flagged down a police car and told them I had hit her and was trying to rape her." (The charges were dropped three days later.)

Some neighborhoods in San Francisco are "contested zones," areas that the rabble want to use and the police want to clean up. In these contested sections, police enforce stringent standards against the disreputables. Seven of the arrests made in contested zones were for behavior by disreputables that probably would have been tolerated in rabble zones. For example: "I was walking through the Haight [a zone that is rising out of its mid-1970s depths as a hippie skid row], and a police officer came up to me and asked if I could get him some drugs. I knew he was a cop. Then he wanted me to work for him, turn in people I knew who were dealing. I wouldn't, so they busted me." (The charges were dropped by "order of the court" when this man appeared at arraignment.)

Another example: "I was sitting on the steps at Walgreen's on Polk Street [a contested neighborhood] drinking vodka. The police came up to me and told me to pour it out. Then they searched me and found some grass on me. It was less than an ounce. They arrested me for possession for sale." (The charges were reduced in court to a misdemeanor and the man fined $100.)

When police see disreputables in respectable neighborhoods, they watch them closely and apply very strict standards. In our sample of 100, thirteen rabble types were arrested in respectable neighborhoods for committing acts that probably would have been ignored if they had occurred in rabble zones or if reputable people had committed them. One of the thirteen reported: "I was riding around with a friend and his car broke down. He got out to fix it, and across the street some guy ran away from an open car. We went over to look at it and were looking in the window when the cops pulled up. They arrested us for burglary." (The charge was dismissed the next day.)

Raids

In addition to containing deviance within rabble zones and acceptable limits, police officers, particularly members of the vice squad, make raids into the zone to arrest particular individuals or types of disreputables. Raiding Tenderloin hotel rooms and apartments to capture persons involved in drugs is the most common form of raid in San Francisco. Nine of the felony arrests in our sample were apparently the result of raids. For example, one interviewee said: "We were in our room in a hotel on Eddy Street [in the Tenderloin] and the cops came busting in the door. They were undercover narcotics agents. They started hassling everyone. There were a lot of drugs in the room. They arrested everyone. They told me, 'We're sending you back to San Quentin.' "

Another common form of raid depends upon the use of "plants" to catch petty thieves on the street. A booking report read:

> On Tuesday 11-17-81 at 13:15 hrs. Lieutenant B. strolled east on Market Street. Lt. B. feigned the appearance of an elderly pensioner, and in his right rear pants pocket was a tan envelope containing $2.00. Lt. B. stopped and looked eastward when R. approached Lt. B. and took the tan envelope out of the pocket. R. was arrested by Sergeant W. and transported to the Hall of Justice where he was booked on the above charge.

Sweeps

Occasionally the police set out to round up an entire category of rabble in order to clean up the streets in an area. For example, the Las Vegas police went after street prostitutes in March 1981. "Almost 300 prostitutes were arrested and taken to jail during the first 48 hours of a police crack-down on Las Vegas Strip prostitution, Assistant Sheriff Jere Vanek said yesterday. . . . 'The street hookers are offensive, have no tact, no finesse, they get into fistfights over turf.' "[43]

In Miami in October 1982 the police swept the streets of derelicts before the arrival of a convention of travel agents. A newspaper reported:

> Like an anxious hostess sweeping dirt under the rug, Miami is whisking its unwanted derelicts into jail and out of sight of a convention of 6,000 travel agents. Police are cramming Dade County's jails with hundreds of derelicts, apparently in hopes that American Society of Travel

Agents conventioneers will return home and recommend Miami to their clients. "This is a one-week clean sweep strictly for ASTA. We wouldn't be doing this under normal conditions," Officer Luis Alvarez said yesterday.[44]

Although sweeps generally produce misdemeanor arrests, three of the persons in our sample arrested for felonies were apparently caught in sweeps. One of them said: "I was in a parking lot on Mission Street and the police came in with a paddy wagon. They were picking up lowriders. They got me for being high on drugs and for possession of stolen property." (The charges were dropped three days later.)

Helping rabble

Some arrests of disreputables are intended as a form of aid. Police officers are among the few—and are sometimes the only—social agents available to the rabble. As Jacqueline Wiseman has written: "The peace-keeping on the Row can be said to be at least secondarily for the benefit of residents, but more in the manner of the parent who disciplines a child for his own good. Most police consider a drunk arrest to be somewhat benevolent."[45] Arrests of this sort are invariably made on misdemeanor charges. In our sample, some of the misdemeanor drunk arrests may have been "for the benefit of the resident," but none of the felony arrests appeared to be for the purpose of extending aid.

Fighting property crime by rabble

One of the most troublesome activities of the rabble class, which the police make a constant effort to stop, is its persistent assault on the private property of respectable citizens. Fifteen of our 100 felony arrests were of disreputables for stealing property from reputable people or businesses. Here are two examples from police reports:

Received a call via radio re: an 852 in progress [theft from auto] in the 2800 block of Jackson Street [a highly respectable neighborhood]. As we drove in front of [street number] Jackson, Officer Q. and I observed the above boosted vehicle parked inside the garage area of [street number] Jackson. The door to this garage was open partially and we were able to see the garage area. We saw M. in the front seat area, and suspect no. 2 standing next to the right-side open door of the boosted vehicle. Custody of M. was turned over to 3F30 day watch.

Victim/reportee L. told me that while he was standing outside of Studio West dance hall, he engaged in a conversation with suspect no. 1. Suspect no. 1 informed him that a friend of his, suspect no. 3, a white female, was without a date and asked him if he'd accompany them and be her escort. Suspect no. 1 opened the passenger door, where L. sat. L. looked up at him and saw what he described as a .38 revolver pistol in the suspect's hand pointing at him. The suspect then said, "Give me your money." L. complied, fearing for his life. L. handed suspect no. 1 his wallet. Suspect no. 1 then told L. to leave the keys to his vehicle and get out. As L. hesitated at this command, suspect no. 1 kicked him in the face.

Finally, nine of the felony arrests in our sample seem unrelated to managing the rabble. The behavior in question—which ranged from first-degree murder to possession of cocaine discovered during a drunk-driving arrest—would probably have provoked arrest regardless of who had committed it.

Conclusions

By arguing that arrest procedures and the jail are used mainly to manage the rabble, I do not mean to imply that crime is not an issue. As the foregoing partial review and classification of the 100 felony arrests suggests, the majority of those arrested were in fact guilty of some crime. Rather, I would like to emphasize that the culpability of those persons had what Egon Bittner has called "restricted relevance."[46] That is, they violated standards that are enforced with a great deal of discretion by the police and mainly in order to manage the rabble rather than to enforce the law.

Some of the more serious crimes, such as robbery and assault by one disreputable on another, usually come to the attention of the police because of the social setting and the status of the disreputables. Disreputables commit their crimes in a much more obvious fashion than reputable people, and the police, in performing their rabble management function, are keeping their eye on them and expecting them to commit crimes. Police do overlook a lot of criminal conduct by disreputables. However, disreputables commit an enormous amount of petty crime out in the open, and the police see a great deal of it.

Likewise, when disreputables are arrested for violating the private property rights of respectable citizens, it is because the police are at least as interested in managing the rabble as in enforcing the law. It is not simply the fact of theft that provokes arrest; it is who commits the theft and what type of theft it is. Our society—like its predecessors, chiefly England—has been quicker to criminalize covetous property accumulation by the rabble than by other classes. The police are always on the lookout for purse-snatching, theft from cars, and shoplifting, but they almost never patrol used-car lots or automobile repair shops to catch salesmen or repairmen breaking the law, and they never raid corporate board rooms to catch executives fixing prices. The difference between these crimes is not seriousness or prevalence; it is offensiveness, which is determined by social status and context.

2

Who Is
Arrested?

THE VAST MAJORITY of the persons who are arrested, booked, and held in jail are not charged with serious crimes. They are charged with petty ones or with behavior that is no crime at all. And the jail, unlike the prison, has little to do with serious crime. Its primary purpose is to receive and hold persons because they are "offensive." These conclusions are based on an analysis of two samples of a jail's intake population: 100 felony arrests and 100 misdemeanor arrests randomly selected over a one-year period from the booking record of the San Francisco City and County jails. My research assistant and I were not able to interview the persons in the misdemeanor sample because so many of them were released within a few hours of arrest. But we were able to interview all persons in the felony sample within twenty-four hours of their arrest. We questioned them about their social backgrounds, their recent activities, and the circumstances of their arrest, including the nature of the behavior that led to it. In most cases the accounts of events that led to their arrest were patently valid. (Either they openly admitted the truth of the charges, or they denied them and their accounts were validated by immediate dismissals.) But whenever we had any reason to doubt the truth of an account, we sought verification in the court records, the booking reports, and the state's crime records.

Table 1 *Distribution of Charges in the Felony Sample (100 arrests)*

Narcotics law violation	30	Forgery	3
Burglary	14	Rape	2
Assault	12	Murder	1
Grand theft	10	Fraud	1
Auto theft	5	Gambling law violation	1
Unarmed robbery	5	Child molesting	1
Receiving stolen property	5	Attempted murder	1
Armed robbery	4	Weapons law violation	4
		Drunk driving	1

Note: This distribution of charges compares closely with the distribution of arrests nationwide, which indicates that this San Francisco sample is not notably skewed; for a distribution of the major crimes from the records compiled by the Uniform Crime Reports Section of the FBI, see James Eisenstein and Herbert Jacob, *Felony Justice*, p. 14. It does vary slightly from samples of arrests in other cities: New York is higher on robberies, Baltimore on robberies and burglaries, Chicago on heroin offenses, and San Francisco higher than all three of these cities on total narcotics arrests. On the whole, however, this sample roughly corresponds to the other cities' arrest patterns; see Vera Institute, *Felony Arrests: Their Prosecution and Disposition in New York City's Courts*, p. 5; and Eisenstein and Jacob, *Felony Justice*, p. 104.

Crime Seriousness

The distribution of charges in the felony and misdemeanor samples are shown in Tables 1 and 2. (In cases involving multiple charges only the most serious charge is listed.) The misdemeanor charges, of course, were by definition made for crimes that were not considered serious. On the other hand, many of the felony charges pointed to crimes that would be committed only by persons who fit the popular and official conceptions of the dangerous criminal: fourteen burglaries, four armed robberies, twelve assaults, one murder, two rapes, and ten grand thefts. However, these are only the charges made by the arresting officers at the time of booking. They are insufficient for judging seriousness, and there are three reasons why they might be very misleading: the variety of acts that fall within a crime category is great, the police often charge persons with crimes much more serious than their actual behavior warrants, and sometimes the charges are totally fabricated.

To form a more accurate estimation of seriousness, I began by

Table 2   *Distribution of Charges in the Misdemeanor Sample (100 arrests)*

Drunk (or "stoned")	29	Disturbing the peace	2
Drugs	5	Concealed weapon	2
Drunk driving	18	Drug paraphernalia	2
Traffic warrants	18	Prostitution	1
Other warrants (misc.)	10	Violation of city park ordinance	1
Other vehicle violations	3		
Trespassing	3	Violation of public transit ordinance	1
Petty theft	3		
Battery	2	Open container of alcoholic beverage	1

Note: As was the case with the felony arrests, this distribution roughly compares with the distribution of arrests nationwide; see U.S. Department of Justice, *Source Book of Criminal Justice Statistics*, 1981, p. 338. San Francisco is a little higher on the combination of drunkenness and disturbing the peace (or disorderly conduct, as it is listed in the *Source Book*) than the national sample (it is only a sample because of incomplete reporting). On all other charges, my sample is within two or three percentage points of the distribution of arrests nationwide.

studying the descriptions of the crimes given to me in the interviews; then I examined the court records and police reports relating to the cases. For a standard of seriousness I turned to a national survey of crime severity conducted in 1980 by the Center for Studies in Criminology and Criminal Law at the University of Pennsylvania.[1] In this survey 52,000 respondents nationwide evaluated the relative severity of crimes by assigning a numerical score to a short description of each of 204 criminal acts listed in a questionnaire. For example, two of the acts described were "a person steals property worth $10 from outside a building" and "a woman engages in prostitution." The center reduced the total scores given to each of the acts to ratio scores. The scores, being derived from the judgment of a very large sample of Americans, serve as excellent relative measures of crime seriousness—which is ultimately a matter of subjective public judgment.

When the acts of a member of my felony sample closely corresponded to one of the 204 acts described in the survey, I assigned the sample member the survey's score for crime seriousness. But in most cases this could not be done: the acts that led to arrest in my sample did not correspond closely enough to any acts listed in the survey questionnaire. In order to deal with these, I selected similar acts from the survey and read them and their ratio scores to my classes in sociology (about 100 students in all); I instructed my students to use the survey's ratio scores as a scale of seriousness and to give the acts by the men in my sample a score on this scale.[2] After the student scores were averaged and the averaged scores assigned to the remaining men in my sample, the 100 felony arrests had the scores shown in Table 3. Although the lines between crimes that classified as petty (0 to 4.9), medium (5.0 to 9.9), and serious (10 and above) are somewhat arbitrary, they do help define three qualitatively different classes of crime. Petty crimes involve at most a small amount of money and no injury. Medium crimes involve some other element, such as taking a large sum of money, breaking into a house, or using strongly stigmatized drugs such as heroin (heroin use received a score of 6.54 in the center's survey). Serious crimes involve injury or possess some other reprehensible quality; for example, enticing a minor into a car for immoral purposes received a score of 25.72 in the center's survey.

Table 3 demonstrates that seriousness of crime was not a major factor in the arrests: the large majority of the felony arrests fall into the petty category, and seven have a score of zero; the median score is 3.0. Three of the crimes from the felony sample with a score of approximately 3.0 were as follows:

> J. was standing outside a residence "stoned" on drugs and injured from a fight. (He said: "I had just been beat up.") The police pulled up, searched him, and found amphetamine pills in his pocket. They arrested him for public intoxication and possession of dangerous drugs. He received a severity score of 2.5.

> A. was caught leaving an expensive men's clothing store with a shirt priced at over $200. He was arrested and charged with grand theft. He received a score of 3.0.

> M. and a friend left M.'s house to find a part for M.'s wife's car. They found a similar model car a few blocks away and were breaking into it to steal the part when they were caught by the police. They were both drunk. M. received a score of 3.5. ("A person

Table 3   *Crime Seriousness*

Petty	Medium	Serious

```
        X
        X
        X
        X
        X
        X
      X X
      X X
      X X X
      X X X
      X X X
      X X X
      X X X X
      X X X X
  X X X X X|X
  X X X X X|X
  X X X X X|X
  X X X X X|X
  X X X X X|X X
  X X X X X|X X
  X X X X X|X X       X
  X X X X X|X X X X X
  X X X X X|X X X X X        X       X       X       X

  0 1 2 3 4 5 6 7 8 9 10      15      18     25.2    35.7
```

Note: The scores assigned to five acts in the national survey of crime severity, conducted in 1980 by Marvin E. Wolfgang, Robert Figlio, and Paul Tracy for the Bureau of Justice statistics, give this distribution some comparative meaning:

1.14   A person disturbs the neighborhood with noisy behavior.

4.93   A person snatches a handbag containing ten dollars from a victim on the street.

10.27   A person threatens to harm a victim unless the victim gives him money. The victim gives him $1,000 and is not harmed.

30.04   A man rapes a woman. Her physical injuries require hospitalization.

breaks into a parked car, but runs away when a police car approaches" received a score of 3.62 in the center's survey.)

Offensiveness

My interviews and observations in the jail convinced me that in the making of arrests, offensiveness of acts is a more important factor than crime severity. Offensiveness is a definition that conventional witnesses or their agents (the police) impose upon events; it is a summation of the meanings they attach to the acts, the context, and, above all, the character of the actors. When a given act is performed by a disreputable—a person who is deemed worthless or of low character—it is not considered the same as when it is performed by an ordinary citizen. Thus, "horsing around" on a street corner is seen quite differently when it is done by "clean-cut" white teenagers or by "rowdy" black teenagers. A group of Hollywood celebrities and their followers snorting cocaine in an expensive Malibu Beach home is not seen in the same way as a group of lower-class Chicanos shooting heroin in a skid-row "shooting gallery."

An example from my own experience also illustrates the part that imputation of character plays in constituting offensiveness and in precipitating arrest. My wife and I were attending a play at a theater in downtown San Francisco on the edge of the Tenderloin, a neighborhood populated by many types of disreputables—prostitutes, drug addicts, petty hustlers, and derelicts—as well as poor people, most of them elderly. At intermission the audience spilled out of the crowded lobby onto the sidewalk—in fact, slightly beyond the curb onto the street. Many, myself included, had purchased an alcoholic beverage in the lobby and were drinking openly on the sidewalk. If even a small group of Tenderloin denizens had been doing what we were doing—blocking traffic and drinking in public—it would certainly have provoked some action by the police. But when two police officers approached us on foot, they stepped into the street to get around us and walked by.

It is essential to distinguish between seriousness and offensiveness, even though they usually appear together. In the national survey of crime severity, the descriptions of the crimes included no information about the character of the offender and said very little or nothing about the context. If the same 204 crimes had been presented with full descriptions of the persons who performed the acts and the contexts in which those acts occurred, the scores would vary according to the perceived values of these additional aspects.

Repeated examinations of the 100 interviews taken from our felony sample revealed several common types of offensive acts that are likely to result in arrest if they are witnessed by the police or brought to their attention.[3] These types may be ranked as follows according to degree of offensiveness:

Mild: (1) Disreputable person is too blatant in his display of deviant behavior in neighborhoods where disreputables live and congregate (such as skid rows). Examples of "too blatant" deviant behavior would be openly selling marijuana, bothering reputable persons with repulsive behavior, being excessively loud and disorderly, or drinking on the street. (2) Disreputable person shows lack of respect or in some other way challenges the position or authority of police officers. (3) Disreputable person is in a respectable neighborhood where he "doesn't belong" and thereby threatens conventional citizens who reside or do business there.

Moderate: (1) Disreputable person commits a crime in a location where he does not belong (such as a "nice" hotel). (2) Disreputable person injures another disreputable person. (3) Disreputable person fights with police.

High: (1) Disreputable person commits a face-to-face crime against a reputable person.

The 100 felony arrests in our sample were distributed as follows among the three categories of offensiveness: sixty-one mild, twenty-eight moderate, ten high (one not offensive).

The two measures, seriousness and offensiveness, obviously interact: persons fall into a higher category on the offensiveness scale for committing many of the crimes rated serious. In our sample the two variables interact in the manner shown in Table 4. Most cases would fall roughly on a diagonal from the upper right to the lower left, indicating that offensiveness and seriousness vary together. Obviously, however, the sample sags toward offensiveness (on a diagonal from upper left to lower right). Seven cases with some offensiveness had no seriousness (the persons were doing nothing illegal at the time of ar-

Table 4 Relationship Between Crime Seriousness and Offensiveness

Offensiveness	Seriousness			
	None	Petty	Medium	Serious
None			x	
Mild		xxxxxxx		
		xxxxxxxxxxx		
		xxxxxxxxxxx	xx	
	xxx	xxxxxxxxxxx	xx	
	xxx	xxxxxxxxxxx		
			xx	
		xxxx	xxx	
Moderate	x	xxxxx	xxx	xx
		xxxxx	xxx	
			xx	
High		xxx	xxx	xx

rest), but there was only one case with no offensiveness (it was a case of medium seriousness).

Types of Disreputables

In most cases, what first attracts the attention of witnesses, police officers, and victims—what precipitates the arrest of an offender—is the offender's disreputability. His disrepute is not seen as a single quality, however, but as a configuration of attributes that constitutes a "type" of person. Most of these social types are relatively well known by the disreputables themselves, as well as by conventional people (particularly police officers) who have frequent contact with them. Our sample of 100 felony arrests yields the following types, with the number of arrests for each type given in parentheses.

Petty hustlers (28)

Urban skid rows, "tenderloins," and ghettos harbor many disreputables who consider themselves hustlers. They spend large portions of the day on the streets trying to steal or con enough to live on and pay for their pleasures; their testily asserted deviant values weakly support their criminal activities and bolster their dignity. Among disreputables, they are the most bothersome type and the most vulnerable to arrest. This is because their criminal pursuits are highly visible and noticeable, petty and unsophisticated, and threatening and repulsive to ordinary citizens. For example, they sell small amounts of marijuana (five-dollar bags or bogus substitutes) to anyone passing by; or they roll drunks, snatch purses, shoplift, and burglarize cars. In addition, they are on the streets at all hours and are often easily identifiable by their clothes, hair, mannerisms, and speech. Several examples taken from descriptions of the twenty-eight petty hustlers in my felony sample will illustrate this lifestyle and its typical crimes:

> R. is a thirty-eight-year-old white man. He finished the eleventh grade. He says: "I've been hustling all my life." He lives in the Tenderloin, a neighborhood filled with petty street hustlers, and currently tries to make a living selling bogus hash to strangers around Union Square (the center of the downtown shopping area). He has been arrested six or seven times for this activity in the last couple of years. This time he had sold some bogus hash to a man, and immediately two plainclothes police officers arrested him. They charged him with three marijuana felonies: possession, sale, and possession for sale. The next day in municipal court the first two charges were dropped, and he was cited for possession for sale and released. A week later the remaining charge was reduced to a misdemeanor, and he pleaded not guilty. He failed to appear at his next scheduled hearing, and a bench warrant was issued with a bail of $100, which he was given the option of posting and forfeiting as a fine if he was rearrested.

> V. is a thirty-six-year-old Mexican-American raised in San Francisco. His father was a barber and his mother a cook. He did not complete high school. When he was nineteen, he was sent to prison for assault with a deadly weapon, and when he was in his twenties, he was sent to prison for burglary. For the last few years he has been living in the South of Market area, a skid row. He has not worked

for years. His only job skills are landscaping and welding, which he learned in prison. At 8 P.M. one evening he was arrested on Mission Street near Sixth Street, in the heart of skid row. The police officer told him he saw him "messing with the coin machine" in a coin-operated parking lot on Mission Street. The police officer searched him and found ten one-dollar bills. He also found a piece of wire on the sidewalk. He booked him for receiving stolen money, trespassing, possession of burglary tools, and petty theft. V. says that the police officer, who is also Mexican, had it in 'for him. He says that the police officer once asked him: "What are you doing here on Sixth with all these niggers? Aren't you proud of what you are?" Two weeks later all charges were dismissed "in the interests of justice."

H. is a twenty-six-year-old black man. He finished high school and has worked off and on since then in auto repair shops as a body and fender man. He is living in the Tenderloin in one of the run-down hotels. He says he is down and out, that "my little woman just left me, and they don't give me enough to live on on welfare." He sells bogus marijuana to anyone who will buy it. "Some black dude [who turned out to be a narcotics officer] came up to me and asked if I could get him some weed. I sold him two joints that weren't weed." The officer arrested him for possession of marijuana and possession for the purpose of sale. Both charges were dropped the next day.

Derelicts (14)

Most American cities contain a small but highly visible group of people who are not only detached from organized society but teeter on the edge of physical existence. This group is by no means limited to the skid-row drunks who have received so much research and social agency attention.[4] In recent years a growing number of survivors of the 1960s hippie movement and other drug worlds have joined the urban derelicts. The hobo type so prevalent during the first part of the century is reappearing. Many psychiatric patients who have been dismissed from institutions (often for state and federal budget-cutting reasons) and many others who are avoiding institutionalization now add to our urban derelict population.[5]

Street alcoholics and other derelicts are constantly vulnerable to arrest because of their status alone, that is, for being drunk or vagrant or both. Police policy on whether or when to arrest them varies according to the individual police officer, the current "downtown" policy, how long the derelict has been on the streets, and many other considerations. Although derelicts are usually arrested for misdemeanors, they are occasionally charged with felonies—typically for taking something from the pockets of another drunk (these days, often a police plant), assaulting a person (most often another derelict), trespassing at night (and getting charged with a burglary), or stealing something that the arresting officers estimate is worth more than $500 (which constitutes grand theft, a felony). Fourteen of the 100 persons in the felony sample were derelicts. Our notes on two of them read as follows:

W. is a thirty-two-year-old black man who has had no work for a long time. "Been trying to survive. I'm supposed to get on welfare, but they haven't done my papers yet. Been staying with a buddy." W. estimates he has been arrested about five times. He served a nine-month sentence in Los Angeles for assault with a deadly weapon. "It wasn't nothing like that, though. I was visiting this guy, a lowrider, and we got into an argument. I went back to scare the dude and they busted me." The night of the current arrest he was drinking and smoking marijuana. "I walked out of a poolroom where I had been drinking. I smoked a joint and headed for a liquor store on Ellis and Hyde [in the Tenderloin] to get me a little taste because I had to be out all night. I saw this guy on Turk Street. Some guy had fell off his motorcycle. The police came down to see. They saw a few joints of marijuana on the curb and said it was mine." W. was charged with possession of marijuana for sale. This charge was dismissed several days later, but he was held on violation of probation. After five weeks he was discharged from custody.

S. is a sixty-one-year-old Mexican-American raised in El Paso and Los Angeles. When he was young, "the kids had to work so we quit school." He has not worked for a year. His last job was as a janitor in a housing project. He was arrested "quite a few times" in Los Angeles many years ago, and he served a sentence of 180 days there. The last time he was arrested in San Francisco he "was just walking across the street." This time he was arrested while carrying a rifle to a pawn shop. The police stopped him on the street and asked where he had obtained the rifle. He told them he'd found it in the back of a pickup truck. At first, he said, the police didn't know what to do. "They tossed it back and forth, then one decided to arrest me." The charge of receiving stolen property was reduced to a misdemeanor the next day, and S. was cited out of jail. He pleaded not guilty a week later, and at the next hearing three weeks later the charge was dismissed.

Junkies (6)

Junkies are persons who are or have been addicted to one of the opiates (usually heroin), who continue to use drugs (though not necessarily an opiate), and who identify themselves as drug addicts. The drug life they follow is too chaotic and expensive to allow them to support a habit through conventional employment, so they must steal or hustle.[6] Most police officers immediately arrest junkies when they catch them in some illegality, such as possession of drugs, and narcotics officers keep up a constant campaign against them. There were six junkies in the felony sample.[7] The following was typical in most respects:

W. is a forty-year-old black man raised by his mother in San Francisco. He has been a heroin addict for the last fifteen years. During this period he has been arrested at least twenty-two times. These arrests have resulted in two county jail sentences, a prison term, and several trips to the California Rehabilitation Center, which is the drug treatment prison in California. The present arrest occurred in a motor hotel in a relatively nice residential section of San Francisco. He was seen by police in the halls of the hotel and stopped. When he was searched, they found jewelry and a screwdriver and charged him with burglary. His fingerprints matched those from another burglary. He was eventually charged with three different burglaries. Two weeks later in superior court he pleaded guilty to all charges, and a month later he was sentenced to the state prison for three years.

Outlaws (4)

The police arrest a few people who are real outlaws. This does not mean that they are skilled thieves committed to the old thieves' value system, for that type is rare today.[8] Usually they are persons who have adopted an outlaw identity and perspective (often in jail or in prison where this new identity flourishes). This identity pits its carriers against society and instructs them to commit desperate criminal acts—such as the armed robbery of Mom-and-Pop stores—that have a high risk of injury for the victims and outlaws alike. Most outlaws have served prior prison terms, most frequently for burglary or robbery. Here are descriptions of two of the outlaws in the felony sample:

> S., a twenty-four-year-old Samoan man, was arrested for armed robbery when he was eighteen years old. He was not convicted but spent several weeks in the county jail. For the next few years he worked irregularly, drank, used drugs, and got into fights. In the present arrest he and two female friends went to a dance hall and lured a man into leaving with them in his car. A block away S. pulled a .38 revolver, told the man to "give me your money," and ordered the man out of his car. S. and the two women drove off in the man's car. They were traveling over the speed limit and were noticed by two police officers in a squad car, who chased them until S. crashed the car into a concrete pole trying to turn a corner too fast. S. was convicted of robbery and sent to prison for five years and four months.

> H. is a nineteen-year-old black youth. His father is a boiler engineer, his mother a housewife. He finished the tenth grade. He was arrested for assault as a juvenile and for robbery as an adult. He is on probation for that robbery. He has not been working. He and a friend are accused of robbing a man on the street. As they were walking down the street, the man led the police to him. The police charged him with armed robbery with a gun. The man was robbed of personal property, but no money. H. was found guilty of assault and armed robbery and received a three-year prison sentence.

Crazies (4)

Since the expansion of the rights of mental patients—which led many inmates of mental hospitals to refuse further hospitalization—and the reduction of mental hospital populations for economic reasons, the number of profoundly disturbed and bizarre-acting persons circulating through San Francisco has increased.[9] Occasionally one of them goes beyond (sometimes far beyond) the minimally acceptable standards for public behavior, even in neighborhoods where the standards are not high. For example, "crazies" may trespass in a forbidden area (behind the barriers in a bank, for example), verbally or physically accost strangers, expose themselves, defecate on the street, or destroy property. When they go too far, the police may be summoned and an arrest made. Frequently, felonies are charged, sometimes for resisting arrest. The felony sample contained four such persons, exemplified in the following case description:

J. is a twenty-two-year-old black man. His father and mother worked for the post office in San Francisco. He did not finish high school and has not been able to work. He is being supported by his father's Social Security payments. He has been arrested twice before, once for a felony that resulted in his being sent to the California Guidance Center at Vacaville for psychiatric observation. He reports that on the day of the present arrest he was driving through the Tenderloin with his window down. He thought a man on the sidewalk made a derogatory comment about him. He got out of his car, confronted the man, and knocked him unconscious. While the man was on the ground, J. rummaged through his pockets and took his money. Then he stood there until the police arrived. He was booked for aggravated assault and one count of first-degree robbery. A month later the court moved to determine whether he was mentally competent to stand trial. He was found competent three months later, and he pleaded not guilty by reason of insanity. He was sent to Atascadero, the state institution for the criminally insane.

Corner boys (14)

A marginally disreputable type is the male member of the working or lower class who hangs around with other peers on the street and in other public places, especially bars, in working-class and lower-class neighborhoods. Early in the history of social science studies of urban deviance, this type was labeled the "corner boy."[10] Corner boys are vulnerable to arrest for several reasons. They are on the streets for many hours in neighborhoods that the police regularly patrol. They exhibit working-class or lower-class notions of manhood (particularly by acting tough or mean) that provoke hostile reactions from police. And under special conditions—such as when they are in the company of more criminally oriented acquaintances, saving face in front of peers, intoxicated, or simply given the opportunity for quick financial gain—they may engage in illegal acts. They may get into fights, beat up their girlfriends or spouses, participate in gang rapes, steal something, receive stolen property, or break into houses or stores. Here are descriptions of three of the fourteen corner boys in the felony sample:

J. is a twenty-one-year-old black man who finished high school and has worked as a carpenter's apprentice. He was raised in Tennessee in a family with fifteen children. The father drove cement trucks. At present he is not working for a salary but is a full-time volunteer at the Glide Memorial United Methodist Church and hopes to get on the staff. He was arrested once before, when he was sixteen, for a misdemeanor. On the night of his present arrest he had had a few drinks and was on the street bargaining with a Tenderloin prostitute, arguing with her over the price. "Some guy—her pimp—jumped on me, and I pulled out a knife. They said I cut her. I don't think I did. I ran into the Jack-in-the-Box, and the police were sitting there. They believed her story and arrested me." J. was charged with felony assault and possession of an illegal weapon. The next day the assault charge was dismissed, and he pleaded not guilty to the weapons charge. He was placed on a diversion program.

L. is a twenty-one-year-old native white San Franciscan raised in the Excelsior District, a working-class residential neighborhood. His father is a truck driver. L. quit school in the eleventh grade and works in a furniture warehouse shipping and receiving furniture. He has been arrested once before for being drunk and brandishing a weapon. On the night of the present arrest he was with his brother and some other friends playing pool in a bar in the lower Mission District, a working-class section. His brother and a friend went into the toilet to snort some cocaine. The police were watching this toilet and caught the two with cocaine. They were escorting them out of the bar when L. followed them outside. He asked the police what they were doing with his brother, and they ordered him against the wall and frisked him. More words were exchanged. L. was walking away and said something else (he can't remember exactly what), and one of the police officers became angry. L. says the police officer said "Now you blew it" and arrested him. He was released the next day on his own recognizance. After four appearances in municipal court over a four-month span, the charge of possession of drugs was dismissed.

F. is a twenty-year-old Mexican-American raised in San Francisco. His father is a cook in a Holiday Inn, and his mother is a hotel maid. F. quit school after the eleventh grade and went to work as a warehouseman.He has been arrested for hit-and-run driving and on traffic warrants. He was convicted of the hit-and-run and had to serve weekends in jail for several months. On the day of the present arrest he and some friends had bought some beer and were drinking on a corner in the Mission District. A young girl walked by, and one of his friends talked to her, coaxed her into his nearby car, and "was doing his thing with her when the cops pulled up and asked them what they were doing." The friend jumped out of the car and ran. The police determined that the girl was sixteen and arrested F. and his friends for rape. The charges were dismissed in court the next day.

Lowriders (4)

In the 1950s the term *lowriders* was used by people in lower-class and working-class neighborhoods in Los Angeles to label young persons, usually males, who slouched down in their car seats while driving slowly around in their automobiles. The label was derogatory, and the criticism was leveled at the lowriders' ostentatious and arrogant presentation of self. The term moved from the neighborhoods into California prisons where it was applied to young prisoners who were similarly ostentatious in their public display and even more intentionally antagonistic and threatening. The term has now moved back outside the prison as a label for persons involved with the customized cars that have, among other special features, hydraulic lifts that can rapidly raise or lower the body of the car.

Here we shall use the term *lowrider* to refer to urban types, including customized car drivers and punk rockers, that share four essential characteristics: their activities take place in public, usually on the streets; aspects of their behavioral style are threatening and bothersome, if not dangerous, to conventional witnesses; they intend that these aspects antagonize, and even threaten, others; and some of their behavior is both deviant and illegal, for example, racing cars on public streets, excessive public drinking, disturbing the peace, fighting, blocking traffic, destroying property, and petty theft. Four persons in the felony sample fit this description. Here are our notes on two of them:

J. is a twenty-nine-year-old white man raised in a middle-class home in the Bay Area. His father is a civil engineer. J. finished two years of college. He also served two prison terms and several jail sentences for crimes characteristic of lowriders, such as taking a stolen car across a state line and possession of a gun. He has worked at many jobs, including welding and dishwashing. He is presently living with his wife and another couple in the North Beach area of San Francisco, a district with an intense and relatively seamy street life. From his description, he continues to lead an ostentatiously "wild" life on drugs and alcohol. The night of the present arrest he and five friends were walking down a Tenderloin street. The police, who knew him, approached the group and accused J. of being drunk. He argued with them and then scuffled with one of the policemen. They charged him with attempting to steal the officer's gun and resisting arrest. The charge of resisting arrest was dropped in municipal court, and the charge of attempted grand theft was reduced to a misdemeanor. After forty days in jail he was released on his own recognizance. He pleaded guilty to misdemeanor larceny and received ninety-one days, ninety to be served in an alcohol program.

F. is a twenty-year-old Mexican-American. He was a "wild" youth and was sent to youth prisons several times. He was recently convicted as an adult for assault and served nine months in the county jail. F. hangs out in the Mission District with his lowrider friends. On the night of the present arrest, he and other lowriders were hanging out in a parking lot in the Mission late at night. The police have been trying to drive lowriders out of the neighborhood, and on this night a paddy wagon pulled up and arrested everyone caught in the lot. F. was charged with possession of stolen property and possession of drugs. Both charges were dropped two days later in municipal court.

Aliens (9)

A welcoming attitude toward immigrants—"Give me your tired, your poor, your huddled masses, yearning to breathe free"—has been one of America's traditional ideals.[11] In reality, however, most waves of immigrants have been viewed as inferior and disreputable. They have been excluded from most conventional organizations, denied employment in most occupations, and persecuted by social-control agencies. For the past few decades, Spanish-speaking immigrants have been the target of public disapproval, discrimination, and intense police action. Presently, San Francisco police focus their social-control activities on Mexicans, Central Americans, and Cubans. This attention is directed mostly toward recent arrivals, but some long-term residents and even some Spanish-speaking Américan citizens have received some of the treatment meant for aliens.

Aliens are vulnerable to police scrutiny and arrest for several reasons. They tend to live in neighborhoods, such as the Mission District in San Francisco, that are heavily policed. Many of them hang out in bars and on street corners that are exposed to more police scrutiny. Their culturally alien behavior, such as speaking in a foreign language, is more likely to provoke a hostile police reaction. Some of them engage in behavior—such as drinking, reveling, and fighting in public—that is deviant by conventional standards. And a few of them, particularly those who are most economically hard pressed, commit crimes of theft. Here are descriptions of three of the nine aliens in the felony sample:

G. is a twenty-year-old Mexican who came to the United States a year before his arrest. In Mexico he had worked as an air-conditioner mechanic. In the United States he worked for a while as a house painter, but he was laid off several months ago and has not been able to find work since. Recently he was riding on a bus and snatched a purse from a woman. He jumped off the bus and was arrested several blocks away; there was no money in the purse. While he was in jail awaiting a court appearance for these charges of grand larceny and resisting arrest, it was discovered that he had been out on bail on charges of resisting arrest and battery to a police officer. All the charges were combined; he pleaded guilty to the purse-snatching and was sentenced to one year in the county jail.

M. is a twenty-eight-year-old Cuban who immigrated a year ago. He had been an electrician in Cuba and was working in this country as a construction laborer. He was visiting San Francisco with a friend and riding on a downtown bus. Three plainclothes police officers approached him and began questioning him. He does not understand English and did not know what they said. When the policemen handcuffed him and started to remove him from the bus, his friend, who speaks a little English, asked them what they were doing. They handcuffed the friend also and arrested both Cubans. M. was denied release on his own recognizance but was bailed out several days later. Two weeks after the arrest the charges were dropped because there was "no evidence presented."

J. is a thirty-one-year-old Mexican who has been in the United States for several years. He speaks no English and did not attend high school in Mexico. Here he works as a body and fender man in an auto repair shop. He had been arrested once before for driving without a license. The night of the present arrest he was at a party in the Mission District. He was standing outside on the street and the police pulled up. After some questioning, they searched him and found some pills, which he claimed were not narcotics. They arrested him for felony possession of drugs. The charges were dropped two days later for "lack of evidence."

Gays (6)

A great many gay men in San Francisco are neither detached nor disreputable: they have conventional jobs, own their own homes or businesses, belong to formal organizations, are connected to large and relatively powerful networks of other gay people, are active in politics, and hold public office. However, as a class they are still seen as disreputable by the police and by many other segments of the citizenry, particularly the Irish and Italian Catholics of working-class and middle-class status, who have been active in local politics and have traditionally dominated the city and county civil service ranks, notably the police and fire departments. Gays are seen as disreputables not only because of their sexual preference but because of other aspects of their lifestyle, such as their highly publicized promiscuous sexual conduct in public bathhouses, some of their clothing styles, and their practice of holding hands and kissing other males in public. Some gays are vulnerable to arrest for sexual activities, particularly when the police are attempting to scare them away from one of the public toilets or parks where they meet for sex. Some gays are arrested for possession of drugs, and a few are arrested for assaults and murders that grow out of the homosexual liaisons. Here are our notes on three of the six gays in the felony sample:

> T. is a thirty-year-old white gay male. His parents are "very wealthy." He finished "almost three years of college." At present he is working as a studio manager for a sound company. On the day of this arrest he was at work, getting ready to go out on a job to set up sound equipment, when a neighbor phoned him to tell him that his housemates were being arrested by undercover police. T. stayed at work, and suddenly police arrived with a search warrant. They found syringes and other drug paraphernalia and arrested everyone in the offices of the business. T. was charged with possession of narcotics for sale, maintaining a location for the use and sale of narcotics, and possession of a hypodermic needle. He was released on his own recognizance the same day, and all charges against him were dropped two days later in municipal court.

> A. is a twenty-six-year-old black gay male. He finished high school and has worked since then as a salesman and in construction. He is presently unemployed and has been hanging around the Polk Street "gulch"—an area where gays, punk rockers, and other street people congregate. He was on the street "talking to a friend" when a police officer approached him with his gun drawn. (A. had previously been arrested for possession of a firearm, and the police officer knew him.) The police officer searched him and found a small pistol on him. (A. says the officer planted it on him.) He was arrested, and in two days he pleaded guilty to felony gun possession. Twenty-seven days later he was sentenced to the twenty-nine days he had already been in jail and was placed on probation for three years.

> R. is a twenty-three-year-old white gay male. He quit school in Wisconsin, worked as a food service manager, and then joined the army. When he was released, he came to San Francisco. He was living with a thirty-year-old gay lover. They had been supporting themselves selling "crystal," an amphetamine, to other gays at gay baths. (Some gays use the crystal for their extended sexual activity at the baths.) R. had been shooting crystal for some time, and recently he had been using it for several days at a stretch until he would "crash." He had been having an increasing number of arguments with his lover about this habit. In one of these drug "runs"

their argument heated up and led to a fight, and R. stabbed and beat his lover to death. He continued his run until he finally ran out of drugs and crashed. Then he turned himself in to the police. He was convicted of second-degree murder in a jury trial and was sent to prison for a term of fifteen years to life.

Square johns (6)

Occasionally reputable persons, or "square johns," commit a felony of the type that leads to arrest, such as forgery, grand theft, murder, or possession of drugs (increasingly, cocaine). The crime usually grows out of special circumstances that temporarily beset the square john, as indicated in our notes on two of them in the felony sample:

R. is a twenty-six-year-old white college graduate. He was raised in Marin County, a relatively affluent area, in a wealthy home. His father is a successful international businessman; his mother had been secretary at the Maritime Academy in Washington. R. plays the guitar and has been trying to keep a band together. The evening of his arrest he was playing his guitar in Union Square in downtown San Francisco, an area that the police patrol intensely. Two Moonies (young followers of the Korean Reverend Sun Yung Moon) came up to him and accused him of stealing one of their guitars. The police arrived, believed the two Moonies, and arrested him. Apparently his dress, his guitar, and his presence in Union Square led the police to categorize him as a disreputable. R. claims that they were very abusive to him. He was released on his own recognizance the next day, and the charges were dismissed at his second court appearance, six days after the arrest.

V. is a twenty-six-year-old German furrier traveling around the United States. His mother is a secretary and his father a clerk in Germany. V. finished high school and then entered his trade. He had never been arrested before. He ran out of money and in desperation stole a check and tried to cash it at a bank. He was arrested in the bank and charged with possession of a forged check, forgery, receiving stolen property, and possession of false identification. In municipal court a week after his arrest, all charges except possession of a forged check were dropped, and this charge was reduced to a misdemeanor. He was released on his own recognizance after pleading not guilty. His trial was set two months away, and when he failed to appear for trial, a bench warrant was issued.

Summary

The felony arrests were distributed as follows among the ten types:*

Petty hustlers	28	Gays	6
Derelicts	14	Square johns	6
Corner boys	14	Lowriders	4
Aliens	9	Outlaws	4
Junkies	6	Crazies	4

Since the 100 persons arrested for misdemeanors were not interviewed, they are more difficult to type in the manner used above. However, a sketchy classification is possible. Seventy percent of the misdemeanor arrests were made for being drunk (or stoned) in public, for traffic warrants, or for drunk driving. Interviews of twenty persons in the tanks holding misdemeanor arrests (not the persons in my misdemeanor arrest sample) and my months of observation in that section revealed that the persons arrested for being drunk or stoned were mostly derelicts, corner boys, and petty hustlers. The majority of those arrested for drunk driving and traffic warrants were "ordinary citizens," that is, not the disreputable types that predominated in the felony arrests. However, they were mostly working class and lower class and disproportionately nonwhite. Other characteristics of both samples are summarized in the appendix, which also gives descriptions of the persons who stay in jail and the case dispositions made for everyone in the two samples.

Conclusion

The interviews and follow-up of the random samples of arrestees indicate that the persons who fill the jails in the big cities are largely members of the rabble class, that is, persons who are poorly

---

*Other types have existed in San Francisco in the past and exist now in other locations. For example, my field work at the Los Angeles County jail introduced me to a prominent Los Angeles type: the "gang banger" or "cholo," a member of a black or a Chicano gang. In Yolo County, a rural variation of the corner boy is frequently arrested. During a given time period, every location may have a particular set of disreputables.

Table 5 *Relationship Between Offensiveness and Seriousness of Crime Among Arrestees Held over Ten Days in Jail*

	% Held over 10 Days	No. of Cases
Offensiveness mild, crime petty	33	57
Offensiveness moderate or high, crime petty	16	18
Offensiveness mild, crime medium or serious	20	5
Offensiveness moderate or high, crime medium or serious	65	20

integrated into the society and who are also seen as disreputable. This definition closely fits petty hustlers, derelicts, junkies, crazies, and outlaws. Corner boys are marginal rabble; many of them are in contact with working-class values, and their occupational and judicial fortunes will be critical in determining whether they manage to blend into the reputable working class. Aliens begin on the margins of society outside its culture and social organizations, and in spite of their struggle to enter it, many fail and become permanent rabble. Many low-riders come from solid working-class or middle-class backgrounds and are street people by choice; but continued participation in lowrider activities and its attendant brushes with the law may sever their ties and convert them into full-scale rabble. The gays are similarly marginal. Those with firm ties to conventional society will usually rebound quickly from adverse occurrences, such as going to jail; but others may lose their fragile social positions and take up full membership in the rabble.

The study of the arrest samples also indicates that offensiveness, as much or more than crime seriousness, was what led to being arrested, held in jail until disposition, and then perhaps being sentenced to jail.[12] It also appears that both seriousness and offensiveness must be present to cause a person to be held in jail for more than a few days. The relationship between these two characteristics and being held for more than ten days is demonstrated in Table 5. Finally, receiving a jail sentence was related more closely to offensiveness than to seriousness: 23 percent of the persons with moderate or high offensiveness were sentenced to jail, compared with only 8 percent of those convicted of medium or serious crimes.[13]

3

Disintegration

WHEN THE POLICE bring arrested persons to the jail, their obvious intention is that the "offenders" be held there, tried for their crimes, and then, if found guilty, punished. This is the official purpose of jailing people. But the jail—like most public institutions—has other unstated purposes as well, and these often produce undesirable, unintended consequences.

To understand fully the jail's purposes, we must keep in mind that it is intended to hold the rabble, not other persons. Reputable people commit crimes and occasionally are arrested; but it has never been social policy to keep them in jail while they await trial. Other provisions have always been made for them. As we have seen, when the jail first came into use in England, bail to assure a court appearance was used more often than jail. Today, in addition to setting bail, most jurisdictions systematically release many persons on their own recognizance (OR), and the decision to do so is directly related to reputability.* Recently, many cities have introduced "citation" programs in which police officers may treat some misdemeanor offenses as if they were traffic violations; they may simply issue a citation that requires the offender to pay a fine or appear in court. The decision to cite is usually discretionary, and like all discretionary judicial decisions, it is related

*In programs patterned after the original Vera Institute experiment, as most OR programs are, recommendations are made on the basis of ties to the community. Having continuously lived and worked in the city for a certain length of time and having local residents vouch for one earn a person a recommendation to be released on OR. See Daniel J. Freed and Patricia M. Wald, *Bail in the United States*.

to repute. Consequently, when reputable people are arrested, they are almost always cited, bailed out, or released on their own recognizance. The only significant exception is when they are arrested for drunk driving, for which most state laws require a short period of detention for sobering up.

All persons who build and manage jails assume that the jail is almost exclusively for the rabble. A recent occurrence, described to me by a young woman, demonstrates this understanding:

> They came to my work at the hospital, showed me an arrest warrant for drug offenses, and told me they would have to take me in right then. They were polite, but they told me I couldn't make a telephone call. I said: "I don't care, I'm going to call my husband." They didn't stop me. When we got to the jail, I was so nervous, they began to worry about me. You could tell they all knew I was unusual, different from the other people being booked. I was dressed the way I am now [she had on a smart woman's business suit] and looked like Miss Middle America. One of the deputies, a woman, took me aside and asked me if I could make bail. I told her it would take a day or two. She said I couldn't be OR'ed until Monday. It was Friday evening by then. I told her I *couldn't* stay there. She asked me if I knew any "brass." I said: "Yes, I've got a friend who is a district attorney." She told me to go ahead and use the phone on the desk. I reached my friend, and he told me not to worry, he would have me out of there in a couple of hours. He located a judge at a dinner party and got him to sign the OR release. He came up and sat with me in an office in the jail until the release was processed.

Certain significant physical characteristics and management processes of jails reflect the fact that they are intended to hold only the rabble. First, because many of the rabble are not trusted to appear at their court hearings or even to stay in jail, security has been the fundamental concern in the construction of jails. In the United States this concern almost invariably results in massive buildings, complicated locking systems, and elaborate surveillance techniques, which not only increase security but also restrict the prisoners' movement and form almost impassable barriers between them and outsiders. Second, because the rabble are not expected to behave themselves in jail, they must be controlled. This is partly a concern for the safety of deputies, citizens, and prisoners; it is believed that some prisoners may harm others or destroy property. The concern for control, however, stretches far beyond protecting life and property. It extends to enforcing behav-

ioral conformity for managerial convenience, and even beyond that.
As Hans Mattick has noted:

> Some jail administrators go overboard when it comes to the smaller de-
> tails of jail security. Instead of relying on good peripheral security and
> the rational internal deployment of staff, they deplete the time and ener-
> gies of their limited staffs by harassing the inmates in the details of daily
> living by frequent head counts, strip searches, cell "shakedowns," and
> the censorship of prisoner mail. In general, this is a wasteful use of
> scarce personnel. There is also a general tendency to treat *all* prisoners,
> except "trusties," as maximum security cases, while "trusties" are
> given too much freedom and responsibility because they are the de facto
> operators of the jail. [1]

The concern for control is also expressed in extensive measures to
prevent immoral behavior by prisoners, such as drinking, gambling,
taking drugs, and engaging in sex. Moreover, when officials plan jails,
they go to great lengths to keep prisoners out of sight. For the last two
centuries our society has been removing most problem populations
(such as convicts and the insane) to remote asylums.[2] The jail, however, because of its relationship to the court, must be in or near the
center of the city.* Therefore, prisoners are hidden deep within a massive building. In the last several decades, jail planners have successfully hidden even the jail itself, by placing it out of public view at the
top of a building and disguising its special features (such as barred
windows).

Finally, officials and jail administrators have always assumed that
the prisoners in jail are culpable and generally deserving of punishment. This has been true since jails first appeared in England. Ralph
Pugh, in his history of incarceration in England, makes the point that
"if a man got so far as to be committed custodially to gaol, he must be
a 'criminal type.' Bracton, for instance, declares that a man who con-
fesses to a serious wickedness ought not to be bailed and . . . [implies]
that the wicked ought to be punished with imprisonment even before
trial."[3]

The purpose of punishment not only manifests itself in the structure
of the jail, which has less space and fewer physical resources and material amenities than other "total institutions," such as prisons and

*For sentenced prisoners, as opposed to pretrial detainees, many counties maintain
additional facilities, often farms or camps. San Francisco, Los Angeles, and Yolo counties all maintain additional facilities outside the city.

mental hospitals. It is also expressed in the general management style of the jailers, which is one of malign neglect. The jail's policies and informal custodial practices, and much of the interaction between jailers and the jailed, contain a thinly disguised element of intentional meanness. This is so because most persons who determine jail policy or manage the jail, as well as the general public, believe that jail prisoners are disreputables who deserve to be treated with malign neglect.

Unintended Consequences

One of the consequences of these structural features and processes is that a jail prisoner generally experiences more punishment per day than a convict in a state prison.* Furthermore, this punishment is intended.[4] But several processes that are unintended and socially undesirable also occur. Going to jail and being held there tends to maintain people in a rabble status or convert them to it. To maintain membership in conventional society and thereby avoid a rabble status, a person must sustain a conscious commitment to a conventional set of social arrangements. When persons are arrested and jailed, their ties and arrangements with people outside very often disintegrate. In addition, they are profoundly disoriented and subjected to a series of degrading experiences that corrode their general commitment to society. Finally, they are prepared for rabble life by their experiences in jail, which supply them with the identity and culture required to get by as a disreputable. These processes—disintegration, disorientation, degradation, and preparation—will be examined in this and the next three chapters.

When persons are arrested and jailed, they suffer more than the obvious forms of discomfort and deprivation: sudden interruption of their affairs; instant and total loss of mobility; abrupt initiation into the jail; a subsequent restriction of activities to a very small area; virtual absence of all opportunities for recreation and expression; unavoidable and constant close contact with strangers, many of whom are threatening or repulsive; and a reduced health regimen that can lead to phys-

*This is generally acknowledged by persons who have experienced both forms of incarceration. For example, when I accompanied prisoners being transferred from the county jail to a state prison, we experienced initial elation over our drastically improved situation. Recently a friend told me that his brother had been sent to a state prison but did not want to enter an appeal because it might cause him to be returned to the county jail, which he would do anything to avoid.

ical deterioration and occasionally to serious illness. These discomforts and deprivations are generally well recognized, tolerated, and often intended by jail administrators, other criminal justice decision makers, and most of the public. Officials and the public want prisoners to suffer and to be controlled. But prisoners are more than inconvenienced and deprived. They are extricated and held away from outside social positions and relationships. When these weaken or disappear, future participation and membership in society becomes difficult. I shall refer to these changes as "disintegration." Before examining the experiences that cause disintegration, I must briefly review the requirements for holding a stable position in conventional society.

One requirement is ownership or control over some minimal amount of property—a residence, some clothes, some work tools, and some cosmetic equipment.[5] In our society, of course, almost all conventional persons possess a great deal more than these essentials, which become an issue only when they find themselves without them—as they often do when released from jail or prison.[6]

Another requirement is the presence of some ties to formal and informal social organizations. At the minimum, a person must have some economic ties; he must have a job or some other relationship to a legitimate financial support system. Also, few people can continue to participate in conventional society without ties to families, friends, and social organizations. These social ties do more than provide necessary emotional support and means for expression; they also enable one to accomplish a wide variety of essential goals, such as finding jobs, borrowing money and other property, and bailing oneself out of jail.

A third requirement is the ability to "take care of business." Having a job and a residence and participating in certain social organizations are not enough to guarantee a position in conventional society. People must also actively take care of various formal obligations: they must register their cars, renew their driver's licenses, have their utilities hooked up, and pay their bills, taxes, and traffic tickets.* Persistent

*In 1972 the New York Times ran a story for several days about a young man in Boston who had been living in an apartment without having his utilities hooked up. When the utility company discovered this, it threatened him with arrest, and only after he received considerable publicity and support was an exception made for him. The law, it turned out, requires that residents have utility service.

failure to take care of such business will damage a person's social position.

Loss of property

The deterioration of external relationships often begins at the moment of arrest when persons are immediately and unexpectedly extracted from their normal contexts. To give a common example, if a person is operating an automobile at the time of arrest, the car will be towed to a storage lot. In San Francisco the towing fee is forty dollars, and the daily storage fee is five dollars; after these charges are paid, the auto may be claimed by the owner or someone with a signed release from the owner—but only if the investigating officers have not placed a hold on the car. Holds are often used in drug and property offense cases, and sometimes the officers will not release cars for punitive reasons. To have their cars released while they are in jail, prisoners must obtain a release from the arresting officer, prove ownership of the car, and arrange to have a friend or family member pay the fees and pick up the car. As a caseworker for prisoner services, I once tried to arrange this for a prisoner who was awaiting trial. My field notes on this experience suggest the difficulties.

G. asked me to find his car, get his pink slip (proof of ownership), and deliver the slip to a friend who could then pick up the car. After several phone calls I located the car, but I was informed that it had a hold on it. After several more calls I reached the officer who had placed the hold, and he agreed to sign a release for the car if someone with proof of ownership or a release from the owner would come to his office. The prisoner gave me a signed release for the pink slip, and after several phone calls and two trips to the jail's property room, I found the slip in his wallet. Later that day I delivered the slip to a friend of the prisoner at the friend's home. It would be this person's responsibility to meet the officer (which was going to be difficult because they both worked the same hours), pay the fees, pick up the car, and then hold it for his jailed friend. Several weeks later I saw the prisoner and asked him about the car. He told me that he never got it out of impoundment and that he now owed more than the car was worth.

Similarly, prisoners who are renting rooms or apartments may fall behind in their rent while they are in jail and become subject to eviction. Few jail prisoners own real estate, but a fair number are making payments on automobiles and less expensive items of personal property, which they often lose when they fail to make their payments.

Prisoners often lose clothing and other personal property left in cars or rooms at the time of arrests. When James Spradley asked a sample of persons arrested for public drunkenness how often they had lost property or clothing left behind in their rooms, they reported as follows: many times, 31 percent; occasionally, 20 percent; and at least once, 23 percent.[7]

In most jails, prisoners' street clothes are taken from them, and they are issued special jail clothes. Their own clothes are kept in a clothing room and returned to them for court appearances or release. But the clothes are often guarded with little care and are sometimes misplaced or stolen.[8] The following incident described in my field notes suggests the general lack of concern shown by deputies for the property of prisoners. A prisoner reported to me that he had been transferred briefly to the county jail in the adjacent county to make a court appearance. In accordance with the policy in San Francisco, his street clothes and money were sent with him. When he was transferred back to San Francisco a few days later, the clothes and money were not sent back with him, and he asked me to retrieve them for him. I phoned the jail in the adjacent county several times and finally reached a deputy who was in charge of these procedures. He said it was against his county's policy for him to return the clothes or money; the prisoner or someone with a signed release would have to come to pick them up.

Loss of social ties

Upon arrest, persons are immediately separated from the society outside. While they are in jail their communication with friends, employers, creditors, and organizations is almost entirely cut off. Spradley has written that the drunk tank "cuts the tramp off from the rest of society by setting up an almost impenetrable communication barrier between those in the tank and those outside."[9] In fact, this happens to virtually all prisoners, and the communication barrier stays in place throughout their incarceration.

Legally, prisoners have the right to place two calls at the time of arrest, and the courts have ruled that they also have the right to place calls during their period of detention. In practice, however, these rights are extended with considerable inconsistency and arbitrariness, and prisoners usually have great difficulty communicating with outsiders by phone. At the jails in San Francisco County, prisoners are permitted to use a pay phone in the booking area for two calls after they have been booked. If they have money in their possession, they may use it; if not, they are given a dime and they must phone collect. After the booking process is completed, making calls becomes more difficult. In County Jail No. 1 there are pay phones in every tank, though again the prisoner must have money or call collect. In County Jails No. 2 and No. 3 (which hold only male prisoners) pay phones are brought to the tanks about twice a week, at some time during the day or early evening. No telephone directories are provided. All calls must be made collect. Calls can be placed only during the short time when the phone is at the tank, and prisoners must hurry their calls because others are waiting to use the phone. In effect, their communication by phone is severely limited and strained.

In County Jail No. 1, where jail prisoners are placed immediately after arrest, visits are permitted every day between 11:30 A.M. and 2:30 P.M. They are restricted to about twenty or thirty minutes; the visiting room is crowded and noisy; and the visitors and prisoners are separated by thick glass and talk over a phone. At County Jails No. 2 and No. 3, to which prisoners are transferred after their cases have been remanded to the superior court or they have been sentenced, visits are restricted to two days a week. At No. 2 they are conducted through glass and over the phone; at No. 3 they are conducted through two layers of thick screen that reduce visibility and sound considerably. Visitors at all three jails are inconvenienced and made uncomfortable. At the two downtown jails, where visitors must arrive early if they want to be assured of a visit, they must wait their turn sitting in uncomfortable chairs or standing in a crowded room. County Jail No. 3 is fifteen miles from the center of the city and cannot be reached by public transportation.

Most of the prisoners who remain in the jail have no money and therefore cannot purchase envelopes, paper, and stamps. Occasionally, writing material can be obtained from other prisoners, but it is seldom sufficient to meet their needs. At the jails in San Francisco County, the prisoner services workers received 500 stamped envelopes a month to distribute to indigent prisoners. We tried to deliver one envelope a week but always ran out before the month ended.[10]

Cut off from their normal "grapevine" and without even a telephone directory available, prisoners are almost completely dependent upon others for the communication required to maintain their positions and relationships in the outside world. But prisoners usually have trouble finding persons with sufficient resources and resolve to help them. Family members—when they are present, willing, and have the resources—do the best; private attorneys, when adequately paid, can accomplish some things; and occasionally salaried or volunteer jail social workers (such as prisoner services caseworkers) help a little. (In my experience the most frequent request made to prisoner services was to convey messages from prisoners to outsiders.) However, the efforts made by others usually fall short of preventing the deterioration of a prisoner's ties to outside organizations. With few exceptions, persons who are held in jail lose their jobs and fall behind or are dropped from school. Among the alcoholics Spradley interviewed, 62 percent said they had lost a job at least once because of going to jail.[11] Such occurrences also tend to reduce a prisoner's future opportunities. The family ties of the prisoner are also weakened. To maintain a stable position in a family, one must meet certain obligations and expressive needs. My study revealed that most prisoners had not been doing too well at meeting their obligations before their arrest, but many had certainly been doing better than they could in jail. Except in the rare cases in which the prisoner has some money of his own, all of his financial obligations are transferred to spouses, parents, or other family members. Occasional collect calls and sporadic letters, and short, noisy, and uncomfortable visits in jail are a feeble substitute for direct contact in meeting the emotional needs of spouses, children, parents, and siblings. And of course the prisoner's arrest itself may cause some family members to feel ashamed and disgusted. Thus, prisoners' positions in their families usually deteriorate.*

Friendship networks, too, must be given constant attention, or they may disintegrate quickly because they lack the strong obligatory ties and emotional bonding that exist between family members. One case in which I was involved during my tenure as a caseworker demonstrates this. A young man who had been in jail for about a week told me

*The exceptions occur when the activities engaged in by the prisoner before he was jailed, such as drug or alcohol abuse, were seriously damaging to his family ties and other relationships, and the jail stops these activities and allows his relationships to stabilize. The question is, which is the more deleterious, jail or the outside activity?

that a group of his friends had raised the money to pay a bail bondsman and that all he needed was a property owner to sign the bond. He gave me the name of an uncle who owned property, the name of a "close friend," and the phone number of a bar where the friend could be reached. He wanted me to bring the uncle and the friends together so his bail could be posted. I phoned the uncle, informed him that a group of the prisoner's friends had raised the bondsman's fee, and then tried to reach his close friend. After several calls to the bar over a two-day period, I finally reached him, and he informed me that the group no longer had the money. My impression was that this man and the other friends were rapidly losing interest in the matter. I explained this to the uncle, and later he paid the fee and arranged to bail out his nephew.

Loss of capacity to take care of business

Incarceration prevents prisoners from "taking care of business" in the usual ways, with resultant damage to their private affairs. Ironically, it also prevents them from taking care of other judicial business so that sometimes their legal position worsens. Many persons held in jail have charges or citations against them pending in other jurisdictions. The courts themselves in these other jurisdictions have the authority to request the transfer of prisoners for purposes of attending court hearings; but a prisoner who has not yet been sentenced cannot arrange this transfer on his own initiative. (On the other hand, if he has received a sentence and has at least sixty days to serve on it, California law provides a procedure through which he may force the other jurisdiction to transfer him for hearings or drop the charges.)

The prisoners who have charges pending in other counties usually try to have the prisoner services caseworkers "clean up" these matters. (This was the second most frequent request received by prisoner services caseworkers.) Unless someone representing the prisoner, preferably an attorney, appears at the scheduled hearings and secures a postponement, bench warrants are issued. These are fed into a statewide communication system and "holds" are placed on the prisoners. To remove these holds, caseworkers must persuade the appropriate officials (usually persons in the prosecutor's office) to drop the charges, withdraw the bench warrant, and notify the San Francisco jails that this has been done. When the prisoner services caseworkers in San Francisco tried to accomplish these things by phone and correspondence, they were usually unsuccessful. Even if the charges were dropped and the warrants lifted, the other jurisdiction often failed to notify San Francisco, and this sometimes delayed the prisoner's release for several days.[12]

Occasionally, this unintended penalty even falls on prisoners who have charges pending in the same county. For example, during my research a prisoner informed me that before his arrest he had been scheduled for a probation revocation hearing in a San Francisco superior court. He wanted me to find out if the jailers would take him to the superior courtroom to make his appearance. I discovered that the county court system's processes of record keeping and communication would have resulted in his not appearing and a bench warrant being issued. I asked a county court clerk to store in the computer the information that the prisoner was in jail and would have to be brought from the jail to the courtroom in order to attend the hearing, but I was told there was no way to do this. I went to the bailiff in the courtroom at which the prisoner was scheduled to appear, and the bailiff wrote the information on his desk calendar so that he would remember to phone upstairs to the jail on the day of the hearing.

Picking Up the Pieces

Some prisoners are released immediately after going to a court hearing if the charges against them are dismissed—and they may hope for or expect such a release.[13] But the majority are released with no advance warning and abruptly thrown back into the outside society. They walk out of the jail into the city at all hours. There is no one to meet them. Most of them have no money, or very little. Their personal belongings, which were taken from them at the time of arrest, have been stored in a "property room." If they are released during the day when the room is open, they may retrieve their property immediately. Otherwise they must come back for it during the prescribed hours.

Unlike released convicts and mental patients, they have received no official preparation for their release.[14] And when they do get out, city, county, and private agencies rarely offer them any help in coping with the problems of reentering society.[15] In trying to pick up the pieces of their shattered lives, most of them will be working alone, with virtually no resources and many handicaps.

4

Disorientation

T HE PROCESS of being arrested and held in jail often produces a profound state of internal disorganization and demoralization. This state is the opposite of "having it together," a popular metaphor for an internal discipline, a spirit, and a set of habits that equip persons to cope with the complexities of modern society. (One can be anxious, neurotic, or even borderline psychotic and still "have it together" in the sense meant here.) To maintain a position in conventional society, one must have the motivation to get up on time, keep appointments, find a new job or a new apartment, and take care of all sorts of day-to-day business. If people do not expend considerable continuous effort, their positions will deteriorate. Being jailed tends to dispirit and disorganize persons in a way that makes this style and level of performance very difficult to maintain. This chapter will describe the disorientation that commonly occurs during arrest, booking, and placement in jail tanks and how different classes of people experience this process. It will conclude with a discussion of this state of disorientation.

Arrest

To fully appreciate the shock of arrest, one must first consider the drastic shift in context that an arrested person experiences. Before arrest, a person is free to go where he wants, do what he wants, and say what he thinks. He can also refuse to do all the things not required of him by law. Repeated nonperformance may have serious repercussions—such as the loss of jobs, friends, and spouses—but the limits are broad, and persons regularly decide not to go to work, or to school, or to meetings, or even to meals and get away with it. Within the practical constraints imposed by economic reality and social commitment, then, all free persons in our society have a wide range of choices; regardless of what choices they make, they all understand that they do have them. This freedom of choice, which is taken for granted by all of us, is completely lost at the instant of arrest.

Between the time police officers decide to arrest a person and the time that person is placed in jail—a period that may stretch to several hours—he is completely immobilized and totally at the command of the officers. His every move is directed. He is regularly told to stand, sit, and not talk or smoke. This totally subordinate status and the means of enforcing it are implicit in the law enforcement powers possessed by the police.

Usually the officers can effect this transition from freedom to complete subservience calmly and efficiently, with little more than a display of a professional manner. Most of the 100 persons arrested for felonies interviewed in this study reported that the arresting officers treated them courteously or at least not harshly. However, a variety of elements can make this transition more stressful and traumatic for both the officers and the citizens.

One of these elements, which officers carry into any encounter with citizens, is a concern for establishing authority. Albert Reiss, who directed an extensive study of police behavior, calls this element the unique feature of police work: "Unlike most professionals, who deal with clients who are preprocessed to accept the authority of the professional when he enters the situation, the police officer must *establish* his authority."[1] Jonathan Rubenstein, another student of the police, describes the means the police officer employs to establish authority:

> He must also learn how to establish and express his authority by cajoling, requesting, threatening, "bullshitting them" as patrolmen say, to avoid using force. He must learn to use his body to express with his whole self an authority represented by the appearance he presents; he must learn to use it as a weapon when the occasion demands. He must learn when to mobilize his physical resources and when to let them slumber, allowing his legal power to act for him. In all of his actions he must learn to acquire a quickness, resolution, and decisiveness that urge

him forward when others withdraw. He must be in control of the situation lest it be in control of him.[2]

As this description suggests, police officers use many techniques to
assert authority, and some of these introduce fear and shock into the
arrest.

When police officers feel that their authority is threatened, they are
more likely to act in a less than civil or businesslike manner toward the
person being arrested.* When they sense danger in an encounter with
citizens, the precautions they take to reduce their own risk add much
more stress or trauma to the arrest. They may order persons out of their
automobiles, have them stand at a distance from the officers and the
auto, order them to stand spread-eagle against a wall or auto while they
search them, or even make them lie face down on the ground.

Police officers who are intensely concerned with securing evidence
in an arrest (as vice squad officers usually are) will sometimes do
things that not only increase their own risk but also shock, frighten,
and even injure the persons being arrested. They may break door
locks, break down doors, and grab or even choke suspects to prevent
them from disposing of evidence. For example, two of the persons in
our felony sample reported that police "broke down the doors" of their
Tenderloin apartments in making drug arrests. And a black petty hustler reported: "They came back to my car and got me out to search me.
I had four codeine pills in my hand. One of the cops from the vice
squad or narcotics, I think, grabbed my hand and almost broke it to get
the pills. Then he told me that he was going to take me someplace and
beat the shit out of me."

Police put arrested persons in the back of a police car or van to trans-
port them to the police station or jail. This ride is intended to provide
for officer safety and prisoner security, nothing more. The late political
activist Paul Jacobs, in describing his arrest, gave one example of the
lack of concern for prisoner safety: "I got into the back seat of the
patrol car, and the police officer got in the front. Before driving off, he
fastened his seat belt, and I looked around for seat belts in the back
seat. There weren't any. I asked him, 'Where is my seat belt?' He ex-

*In his study of police behavior, Reiss and his research team found that in more than
half of the encounters between police and citizens in which the citizens themselves were
not deferential or civil, the police "ridiculed or belittled," were "authoritarian or hostile," "brusque or authoritarian," or "hostile or provocative"; see *The Police and the
Public*, p. 50.

plained that there were no seat belts in the back seat, only in the front. I told him, 'Well, you sit back here and I'll drive us.'"[3] In the back area of police vans where prisoners remain, there is a bench on each side but no outside windows. Usually persons are handcuffed, sometimes very tightly and behind their backs, and they are often thrown in with other arrested strangers, which increases the possibility of discomfort and threat. (A Philadelphia study in 1968 revealed that many rapes had occurred in the back of police vans taking prisoners to jail.)[4]

At best, the ride to jail in the back of a police car or van, which can be long and roundabout, is uncomfortable and disconcerting. A twenty-year-old Mexican lowrider reported: "They separated me from the others and put me in the back of the police van with a bunch of fags they had rounded up. They drove around town, going fast then slow, jerking the wagon, and I had to stand up the whole time." This painful ride usually occurs just as the newly arrested person is becoming fully cognizant of his now reduced status, his imminent introduction to the jail, and his future legal problems.

Booking

The arresting or transporting officers deliver the prisoners to the booking section of the jail.* In San Francisco, they enter the jail from a special elevator that travels between the basement garage of the Hall of Justice, in which the jail is housed, up to the booking area on the sixth floor. Upon arrival, the new prisoners are placed in a temporary holding cell. This cell, which can hold several dozen prisoners, has a solid door with a window through which the booking room officers may observe the prisoners. It has a toilet in a corner, a small stainless steel sink, and benches around the walls—nothing more.

Here prisoners wait while the booking procedure inches along. As new prisoners pour in during the busy night hours, the cell becomes very crowded. (County Jail No. 1, where prisoners are booked, receives 120 to 150 new prisoners every twenty-four hours. It has two

*Many jurisdictions have a hierarchy of jails, for example, precinct stations with holding cells, city jails, and county jails. Prisoners may start at precinct stations and then be transferred to other jails. In San Francisco many persons are first taken to police stations and held there for a few hours before being transferred to County Jail No. 1, which was formerly the city jail. In fact, most of the misdemeanor arrests are released from the police stations through citation or bail. In any case, the disintegrating experiences of arrest and booking are not mitigated by a two- or three-staged entrance to the main jail. If anything, they are intensified.

holding cells.) The crowd will include some persons in various stages of drunkenness, some injured and bleeding, and perhaps a few sick and vomiting. A drug addict may be beginning withdrawal, and many of the derelicts will smell of urine, wine, and body filth.

One or two at a time, the new prisoners—or "fish," as they are referred to in the jail—are called out of the cell and directed to the counter to be booked. An officer takes all objects from their pockets, all their jewelry, and usually their belts; he lists these on a property slip and places them in an envelope to be stored in the property room. The items that prisoners may carry with them are very few—typically cigarettes, letters, and an address book. On a card the booking officer enters essential data: name, age, race, physical description, Social Security number, birth date, charges, bail amount, and "holds"; and he pastes onto the card a photograph taken at the counter with an instant camera.

Most arrested persons by now are becoming preoccupied with personal needs and the actions they should be taking. They may be hungry, sick, or in pain; they may feel pressed to contact family, friends, employers, or attorneys. Spradley, writing about alcoholic tramps, described the situation well:

> When a tramp reaches the cement drunk tank he has a great need for assistance. His mind is filled with questions about the threads of his life outside the bucket: Where is my car? Who will notify my employer so I will not lose my job? What will happen to my clothes and other belongings when the room rent is not paid tomorrow? Where are my glasses? How will I explain this to my family and employer? Who will believe I was robbed by the police? How can I get in touch with an attorney? Who could I get to bail me out? If he is going to get information and assistance in answering these questions, he needs help from someone outside the jail. He has other immediate questions which are often more pressing: How can I get a cigarette? What will I do when I start getting the shakes? Will I go into delayed DT's? What's left in my property? Where are my identification papers? Can I get some medicine for my chronic ailments? Can I make a phone call? Can I get a pencil and paper and even a stamp for writing a letter? As these questions pour through his mind, the man in the drunk tank has already learned there will be difficulties in answering them.[5]

If they make pleas to the officers in the booking room (and many of them do, persistently), these are usually ignored or gruffly refused. Booking officers, who must manage this stream of mostly disreputable and often disorderly new prisoners day in and day out, learn to ignore most requests in order to reduce their own discomfort on the job. In addition, they often develop a profound distaste for incoming prisoners, and sometimes express hostility.

After the initial booking and another wait, which can last for an hour or more, the fish are called to the next stage of the passage process—photographing or fingerprinting. Then they move to the back of the jail, into the tanks where they will be housed.

This passage into the San Francisco jail can take up to five or six hours. Most of this time is spent waiting with other new prisoners in some special cell with only the two accommodations, the concrete bench and the open, jail-type toilet—a porcelain or stainless steel toilet with no seat. If a person has cigarettes or can bum them from others, he may smoke. If the size of the room permits, he may pace. He may strike up conversations with others, but he is often rebuffed. This is not an occasion that stimulates small talk; fear, distrust, despondency, and worry fill the room. He may be compelled to maintain a nervous vigil because of his fear of the others. He may rant and rave, but this will eventually provoke sufficient action from the officers in the jail to stop it. He may make pleas to the officers, but these will usually be ignored. If there is room on the benches or the floor, he may sleep or make the attempt. But more than likely he will sit sullenly and quietly.

The booking procedure varies from jail to jail. For example, at the large Los Angeles County jail, into which about 700 new prisoners are introduced every day, it takes much longer and is conducted with much more discipline. Fish arrive in buses at the back of the jail and are placed in fifteen-foot-square cells with open-barred fronts, which hold up to forty prisoners each. Each cell has four stainless steel benches running its length, a toilet, and a washbowl. A cohort of fish remain in a cell until moved to the next stage and another similar cell. In all, they pass through four stages, which takes an average of eight hours. Then they are placed in a large tank, which has benches and beds, where they must wait for classification. They may be in this tank for a day or two.

During the eight-hour passage through initial booking, bath, identification (where fingerprints and pictures are taken), and the clinic, Los Angeles deputies supervise the fish with harsh discipline. They loudly command them to shut up, sit down, move on, walk against the wall, and keep their hands in their pockets while walking from one cell to the next. The men do not mill about in the holding cells; there is not enough room for that. They sit and smoke, if they have cigarettes—which is less likely as the hours pass, because they cannot buy any. Unless they know other prisoners, they usually refrain from anything but minimal conversation. At the end of this slow journey they receive a sandwich and a cup of coffee.

When they reach the large temporary tank, they sleep, mill about, stand by the barred entrance door, perhaps talk to other prisoners, and wait to be called to a room down the hall where they will be classified for their more permanent location in the jail system. During this extended wait they receive the jail's regular meals, but they are excluded from any of its other activities—visiting periods, phone calls, use of the canteen, and the exercise period.

At the other end of the spectrum is the Yolo County jail, which houses only 160 prisoners and receives about seven persons a day; it processes a new prisoner in one or two hours. The smaller scale, the rural orientation of the deputies, and the influence of a relatively humane jail supervisor, who insists that prisoners not be treated with unnecessary harshness, result in prisoners being booked in a less impersonal and more disciplined manner.[6] Prisoners wait in a small cell adjoining the booking desk. A deputy calls them forward to obtain the necessary information for booking. They turn over their property, bathe and change clothes in a small room adjacent to the booking room, and are then moved to a cell where they will be held.

The Tanks

When the booking procedures have finally been completed, the fish move on to their assigned tank. From jail to jail, these tanks vary greatly in size and layout. In San Francisco County Jail No. 1, where prisoners are received, the tanks hold up to twenty men in four cells that open into a central common area. In Yolo, each tank holds ten to twelve men and has a shower, toilets, tables, and a television set. In Los Angeles, the tanks are called modules (a new euphemism). Each module consists of two banks of cells, two tiers high, divided by a glassed-in walkway (the freeway) that runs the length of the tank and allows deputies to observe the prisoners. The top-tier cells hold four men, the bottom ones six. At the end of each tier there is a television room and a day room. The module holds 250 men.

Whatever the arrangement, all jails share certain characteristics. Many prisoners are crowded together into very small living spaces where the facilities are usually limited to bunks, toilets, tables, sinks, television sets, and showers (the television set and the shower may be inaccessible most of the time). Every personal act—sleeping (and snoring), eating, smoking, talking, bathing, shaving, reading, watching television, playing games, and using the toilet—will be done in a group, even a crowd, sometimes with a deputy (perhaps unexpectedly) looking on.

Moreover, whatever the physical arrangement of the tank, the arriving fish are put with a group of prisoners who have been there for a while, some for months. They are the locals, the established residents. The jail's monotony has stimulated their interest in anything new, its poverty has sharpened their desire for any possible material gain, and its sexual limitations may have whetted an appetite for homosexual adventures. They will be sizing up the fish as soon as they enter the tank.

A fish has good cause to be wary. He is moving into foreign territory, much of it claimed by the residents. If he is a stranger to the jail setting, he will lack the knowledge needed to interpret local interactions, and he will not understand the vast repertoire of taken-for-granted responses used by most of the locals in their daily rounds.[7] He probably understands that some prisoners in the unit have exploitative interests in him, but he cannot be sure who; he must wait to learn who is a threat, who is benign, and who may help or befriend him. In this state of ignorance and vulnerability, he will have to find a bunk, then explore the area to find other places where he may linger. Unless there are trusties whose job it is to assign him a bunk—and often there are not—he must find one on his own, at the risk of provoking hostile encounters with other strangers.

To make his situation worse, he is powerless. He may have been allowed one or a few phone calls during the booking process. But now that he is in the tanks, he is helpless again. If he is waiting for an attorney or bondsman to appear, he is likely to wait for several hours.[8] He will not see family members or friends until the first visiting period, which may be days away. And it will take time—hours, days—before he learns how to arrange phone calls, get letter-writing materials, or use the meager resources available in the jail.

In the meantime, he must wait. He may venture tentatively around the tank trying to learn about the routine and the people there, or he may sit or sleep on his bunk—his only relatively secure territory. But even here he is vulnerable to intrusions. He cannot withdraw permanently. Eventually he will have to eat, urinate, defecate, wash, change clothes, or bathe. During all these ordinary activities, many of which he has always performed in privacy, he will be exposed to stares, comments, insults, threats, and offers from the crowd of other prisoners around him.

Differences in the Arrest Experience

When persons of high repute are arrested, their power, prestige, and class connections usually protect them from the abuses and discomforts that accompany normal arrest. For example, in September 1983 Robert Kennedy, Jr., was searched after leaving an airliner at Rapid City, South Dakota; he had been sick on the airplane and evidently was suspected of having drugs. A small amount of powder (which a later test showed to be heroin) was found in his flight bag, but he was not arrested. Four days later the state's attorney, Rod Lefholz, filed charges against him, but he was not arrested then. "Lefholz said he contacted Kennedy's attorney, John Fitzgerald of Rapid City, who assured him Kennedy was in a drug treatment program and that he would make any necessary court appearances. The prosecutor said based on these assurances Kennedy was granted a personal recognizance bond. No court date was set."[9]

If a highly reputable person is actually booked and held in jail, he or she often receives very special treatment. For example, when Jean Harris, the former head of an exclusive girls' school, was held in a jail after her conviction for the killing of the Scarsdale diet doctor, Herman Tarnower, a newspaper reported that she refused to accept jail food and added: "Warden Norwood Jackson said she has been snacking on food brought by her eight or nine visitors and [has] bought tea bags at the [jail] commissary. He said her son David, 30, and his wife, Kathleen, brought her fresh bread Wednesday, which she ate. 'I had a piece with her, so nothing's indicated that she's going to starve herself,' the warden said."[10]

Disreputable but experienced fish, such as ex-convicts or representatives of other frequently arrested rabble types, experience the least discomfort and shock from arrest. They may be withdrawing from

62   DISORIENTATION

drugs or alcohol, and they may be worried about their property and outside ties, but they are familiar with the booking, fingerprinting, photography, stripping, spraying, searching, and redressing. They are prepared for their new powerless status and the slowness of the booking routine. They understand that resisting or making too many requests is futile, even counterproductive. A thirty-five-year-old black petty hustler said: "No, I never give them any shit. If you give them shit, they beat the shit out of you. Everyone knows this. They're looking for a chance to beat the shit out of you." When they arrive at their assigned tank, such prisoners have techniques to buffer the normally threatening entrance experience, such as giving cues that they are experienced and self-assured. Gene Jimenez has described the self-assurance of the seasoned prisoner, whom he refers to as a "hep," in this way: "As he is being 'sized up'—which he is aware of—he is also sizing them up." His experience tells him that "given the jail population's very rapid turnover of inmates, he may almost be assured that his hep competence will ultimately prevail and he will attain his 'proper' status in the tank."[11]

It is persons with no experience of jail and no obvious repute who suffer the most shock and disorganization from arrest. Among them are a few lower-status but respectable square johns, whose repute is not recognized or considered sufficient to influence the process immediately. Roger Martin, who worked as a deputy in the Orange County jail while laid off from his job as an airline pilot, wrote about meeting an acquaintance in jail:

One evening I was passing the drunk tank when an inmate called to me by my proper name. I stopped and recognized him as a successful middle-aged man who was a neighbor of my parents in Arcadia. He was delighted to see me, to recognize someone he knew, even though it was obvious he was embarrassed to be in jail. "How are you, Roger?" he asked. "Just fine," I said awkwardly. "How are you?" "Terrible. I never thought this would happen to me. I just can't believe that I'm in jail." "What happened?" I asked. "I got stopped for drunk driving," he replied. "They said I was weaving all over the center line. I told them I wasn't drunk, but they made me take some tests. They said I didn't pass, and they brought me here." I felt a wrench of sympathy at the misery in the man's eyes as he looked around the drunk tank. He was bewildered and frightened. He had lived more than fifty years without seeing the inside of a jail. Nothing in his life had prepared him for this.[12]

The majority of the less experienced fish, however, are the marginal rabble, usually corner boys or aliens, who have been arrested only once or twice, if ever. They pass through arrest and entrance to the jail without assistance from outsiders, without special consideration from the arresting or booking officers or any other agent, and without much background experience to prepare them. The shock and disorganization they suffer is great.

Self-Disorganization

Internal disorganization begins with the arrest, the drastic transition from being free to being held powerless. It often becomes more intense as the new prisoners are introduced into the jail. Many of them have been arrested after heavy drinking, fighting, or engaging in tension-ridden, physically arduous criminal activities, and during the long, tense journey from arrest to the tanks, they will seldom have received any food (at most, a sandwich and coffee). Their entrance to the jail's main cavities and the approach to the tank where they will be housed can be shocking and frightening. A former prisoner described to me how he felt upon entering the tanks at the Los Angeles County jail:

> I'll never forget it. The place was dim and gray and dirty looking. It had a putrid smell to it. Kind of a mixture of pine oil and dirt. The ceiling was low, and it had little lights that gave off a glow but didn't light up the place. Then I got a good look at the prisoners in the tanks. They were standing around staring at me through the bars. It looked like a concentration camp. Everyone had a sallow look. The white guys, even the Chicanos and blacks, looked gray. Their clothes were dirty. Some of them had scruffy beards. Some of them had no shirts on, others had on dirty undershirts. A lot of them had old beat-up shoes and no socks. Man, it was depressing. Then I realized, in a few days I'm gonna look like that.

During this passage the realization that they have been "busted" for a crime sinks into their consciousness. They face jail, perhaps conviction, and more jail or prison. Sometimes their arrest will expose aspects of their lives unknown to many of their friends and associates, and they will face scandal. Now, sobering up from alcohol, coming down from drugs, or cooling off from rage, they may be feeling regret and guilt for earlier actions.

They also are justly concerned about being harmed or exploited by other prisoners. Some rapacious experienced prisoners in the tanks will spot inexperienced new prisoners and set out to exploit them. Jimenez has described how "lames" and "squares" are fleeced in the Los Angeles County jail: "Sometimes, if lames and squares have indicated on their property slips that they have a full or nearly full issue of money on their persons (and especially if they show a fair amount of money in their accounts as well), they will be placed [by the tank trusties] in front area cells. After the money has been taken from them, either by force or by 'confidence' methods (or both), they will be sent to the rear of the tank."[13]

New prisoners, particularly if they are young and white, are also concerned about being sexually exploited.[14] Though sexual assaults have become much less frequent, they are still a significant element in jail folklore, and inexperienced prisoners are very fearful of them.*

The nature of the disorganization and demoralization that many prisoners experience after being arrested and jailed has not been treated adequately in sociological studies. Sociologists have focused on alienation or anomie; but neither of these concepts, as they appear in the literature, fully or precisely captures the psychological state of confusion and demoralization experienced by many prisoners, especially the less experienced ones. Alienation—with its particular aspects of powerlessness, meaninglessness, normlessness, isolation, and self-estrangement—has referred mainly to a pervasive societal condition or mentality, not to a suddenly induced psychological state.[15] For example, Erich Fromm writes: "Alienation as we find it in modern society is almost total; it pervades the relationship of man to his work, to the things he consumes, to the state, to his fellow man, and to himself."[16] Another student of alienation, Gwynn Nettler, recommends that the concepts of alienation and anomie should "not be

---

*Sexual assaults in jails apparently peaked in the late 1960s; see Alan J. Davis, "Report on Sexual Assaults in the Philadelphia Prisoner System and Sheriff's Vans." My observations and interviews indicate that these assaults are much less frequent now. In the late 1960s more young and inexperienced white males were coming to prison on drug charges, and some of them were sexually exploited by black males who were openly expressing intense hostility toward whites in general and saw the young whites as weak and effeminate. This raping of white "hippies" as an expression of hostility has now become less frequent; and most white youth who are arrested, even if they are inexperienced with jail, have heard about the dangers of being raped and are somewhat better prepared to defend against it. However, the prospect of being sexually exploited is still a very threatening one in the minds of new, inexperienced prisoners.

equated, as they so often are, with personal disorganization defined as intrapersonal goallessness, or lack of 'internal coherence.' "[17] To be sure, Emile Durkheim, the originator of the sociological concept of anomie, refers to the personal disillusionment and suffering that occur when moral constraints are absent, and he attaches these intrapersonal states to sudden changes in persons' social circumstances, such as divorce.[18] Nevertheless, the disorganization and demoralization experienced by some prisoners are more complex and profound than disillusionment and suffering, and the causes are more numerous than the absence of moral constraints or "normlessness" (as American sociologists have translated Durkheim's *anomie*). Jail prisoners, particularly the less seasoned ones, experience all the various conditions that produce alienation. They feel powerless because they are in a restricted, authoritarian situation in which they have few options of any kind and in which most of the major decisions affecting them are made without their input and often without their knowledge. This situation has no meaning for them because they are suspended from activities that have significance according to their own view of the world or their own scheme of meanings. Unless they are experienced, they lack a set of appropriate norms because the moral codes they have known in the outside world, whatever their nature, are not adequate for the jail situation. They are isolated because they are separated not only from society's dominant culture but also from their outside social organizations and networks.*

When all these conditions are applied to the new prisoner in a sudden and intense fashion, they produce the feelings of malaise, anxiety, disillusionment, and despondency that have been associated with alienation. But the dynamics in the situation can produce even profounder states of disorientation. To understand these states, it will be useful to consider the general situation of the "stranger" approaching the social group. Alfred Schuetz, in his 1944 essay on the stranger, introduced us to the array of taken-for-granted understandings that enable us to carry on interactions with others.[19] Following Schuetz's lead, I examined the extreme and profound confusion experienced by

---

*Inside the jail, inexperienced prisoners are also separated from the crowd of prisoners around them. They usually have no acquaintances except possibly the persons who were arrested with them; and in most cases jail deputies separate "crime partners" because they believe that any cohesive prisoner groups are a threat to jail security. Thus, fear and distrust place considerable distance between new prisoners and others.

the recently released prisoner who has lost his taken-for-granted understandings of the outside world:

> Not only does the world seem strange; the self loses its distinctiveness. Not only does the person find the new setting strange and unpredictable, and not only does he experience anxiety and disappointment from his inability to function normally in this strange setting, but he loses a grip on his profounder meanings, his values, goals, conceptions of himself. In this situation, planned and purposeful action becomes extremely difficult. Such action requires a definite sense of self, a relatively clear idea of one's relation to other things, and some sense of one's direction or goals. All of these tend to become unravelled in a radical shift of settings.[20]

If the prisoner is released within a few days, he often is cast back into society in this confused and dispirited state. If he is held in jail long enough to get his bearings there, the transition back into "normal life" can reactivate the confusions. In either case, his ability to get himself and the pieces of his life back together has been impaired.

Persons who are arrested and thrown in jail experience a sudden blow that hurls them outside society. It not only unravels their social ties; it stuns them and reduces their capacity and their resolve to make the journey back into society. One or two blows will not permanently exile most people, but several blows will. It is true that many prisoners were already living outside society's boundaries and that some of them had long since given up trying to move back toward the center. Many of them would come back if the circumstances permitted, but being jailed is not one of those circumstances. It usually propels them further outside. The jail is not the only expelling process, of course; economic misfortune and drug abuse are others. But it is certainly a major one, and this is a cruel irony since its official purpose is to control the behavior of those on the fringe or outside, not to keep them outside or increase their numbers.

5

Degradation

P_{RISONERS} RECEIVE much more than the treatment required to introduce them to the jail and hold them there. They are impersonally and systematically degraded by every step in the criminal justice process, from arrest through detention to court appearance. They are also degraded personally by the hostility and contempt directed at them by police officers, deputies, and other criminal justice functionaries.

Process Degradation

Even when police officers act in a polite and professional manner, an arrest is degrading to all but the seasoned rabble. In making an arrest, officers occasionally invade a person's private space—a home, office, or workplace—and remove him or her from the presence of shocked acquaintances or friends. Most often, however, the police arrest persons in public places where most of the witnesses are strangers; but even this remains humiliating to all but the most hardened and frequently arrested disreputables. Arrests are unusual public events, and those who witness them often express shock, dismay, or revulsion—reactions that further humiliate and degrade the person being arrested.

When arresting officers believe that danger is involved, they often take standard precautions that increase the humiliation. As mentioned earlier, when police fear that suspects may be armed, they make them stand spread-eagle against a wall or hunched over a car hood until they search them. Occasionally, they may go even further. For example, in December 1983 three members of the Harlem Globetrotters basketball team were shopping in downtown Santa Barbara. They left an ice cream store, cones in hand, and hailed a taxi. After traveling for a few blocks through the heart of the business district, their cab was stopped by policemen who ordered them out of the car and commanded them to lie on the ground, face down. A jewelry store had been robbed an hour before, and the police suspected these men—even though their only physical similarity to the robbers was that they were black. Their terrifying and humiliating ordeal, which had drawn a large crowd, lasted until the storeowner arrived and saw that they were not the robbers.[1]

Sometimes persons who are inexperienced or less experienced with arrest and anxious about their suddenly powerless position will argue, joke, or even resist the police, who then respond with tougher tactics.* The total subjugation and immobility that continue through arrest and transportation to jail are deeply mortifying to persons who have never experienced this condition as adults. (Those who have been in the armed services may have experienced something that resembles it in their first weeks after induction.) Erving Goffman stated it well:

> First, total institutions disrupt or defile precisely those actions that in civil society have the role of attesting to the actor and those in his presence that he has some command over his world—that he is a person with "adult" self-determination, autonomy, and freedom of action. A failure to retain this kind of adult executive competency, or at least the symbols of it, can produce in the inmate the terror of feeling radically demoted in the age-grading system.[2]

Degradation increases during the time a person is being introduced to the jail. In his study of "total institutions" (of which the jail is a type), Goffman explored at length the numerous mortifying rituals, such as searching, stripping, bathing, spraying, and the taking of per-

---

*In 1982, F. Lee Bailey, a well-known criminal attorney, was arrested in San Francisco for driving under the influence of alcohol. He pleaded not guilty, and at his trial he testified that he was trying to keep his humor during the arrest by joking in a friendly manner with the police; he said that they became verbally and then physically abusive toward him and that one officer knocked a cigarette out of his hand with a "vicious karate chop." The police officers testified that Bailey was insulting and combative. He was acquitted in a lengthy jury trial. See *San Francisco Chronicle*, April 14, 1982, p. 14, and April 16, 1982, p. 1.

sonal property, that are conducted with the institutional purpose of converting newcomers into manageable inmates.[3] In the jail, since it is conceived by its operators as a short-term holding facility, no elaborate conception of a desired inmate is at work. The jail, unlike other total institutions, is not trying to cure persons or engage them in any complex enterprises, such as running a prison with convict labor. What is needed and wanted in a jail are prisoners who will wait obediently wherever they are placed (in a cell, on a bench, or against a wall), who will make no demands (or few), and who will willingly perform the few required jail procedures, such as returning to their cells, standing for a count, coming to the front when called (for a visit, release, bail, or transfer), and following the procedures required when being delivered to court. Generally the method used to convert free adults into this compliant and passive state is to give commands—either short and polite orders or shouted threats— and to back them up by applying whatever force is required to immobilize a person. This often means removing a prisoner to an isolation cell (sometimes padded) where he can engage in any behavior the surroundings permit without bothering anyone else or damaging any jail property. An example of this regularly and swiftly employed backup force was experienced by Anthony Russo, the co-defendant with Daniel Ellsberg in the Pentagon Papers case. The *Washington Post* reported that Russo wanted to call his lawyer and that after he tried unsuccessfully to get the attention of two deputies sitting outide his door, he protested:

> So I began to yell out through there about how those guys were violating my constitutional rights. . . . I was getting madder and madder . . . and I began to kick the door . . . as hard as I could and these big metal doors make a lot of noise. . . . I did that for about five minutes and all of a sudden the door flew open and a flying wedge of guards came through, four or five and I was flattened . . . they came through, hit me, pushed me up against the wall, said, "Turn around, put your hands against the wall." I did . . . and one hand was jerked away and pushed up behind me really tight. I felt like my arm was going to be pulled out of its socket. And then the second arm was pulled behind me . . . and then someone kicked my legs out from under me. I felt knees all over me, knees on my head, on my neck. I wasn't struggling. . . . They began to chain up my legs, and they put my wrists in handcuffs . . . really tight . . . so they tied my hands cuffed behind me and my legs shackled

together. Then they tied my hands to my ankles, so I was done up in a little neat bow there, lying on my belly.*

The routine demands for compliance, the excessive attention to security, and the general lack of concern for the welfare of the rabble, whom the jail employees understand to be the jail's major clients, result in a painfully harsh introduction to the jail. As we have seen, the fish are herded here and there, crowded together to wait in small, bare cells for unexplained periods of time, and ignored or rebuffed when they make requests; besides being sternly ordered to do whatever is required in the entrance process, they may be commanded to strip naked and bend over with buttocks spread in front of many other fish and deputies.

The degrading experiences and conditions continue during the time prisoners spend in the tanks.[4] Their loss of self-determination becomes only slightly less painful as they learn the official limits and the informal mechanisms for bypassing them. In most jails, they discover that their managers are interested in little more than their name, charge, bail, and court date. Recently many jail systems, such as those in Los Angeles and San Francisco, have also begun to classify incoming prisoners according to a set of custody concerns. Potential troublemakers and "weak" prisoners (those seen as potential victims of exploitation, particularly sexual exploitation) are selected for special placement in tanks set aside for them. Deputies look for any serious medical conditions that might cause a problem while the prisoners are in jail. And sometimes deputies are interested in identifying new prisoners who seem likely candidates for trusty status. Beyond these managerial concerns, the deputies and jail employees have virtually no interest in the individuality of the prisoners.†

In addition, the jail routine makes it virtually impossible for a prisoner to maintain his normal physical appearance, which is a crucial factor in sustaining his conception of self.[5] Immediately upon entering

*Washington Post, Feb. 5, 1972, p. A-6. During my observations of the San Francisco County jails, on several occasions I saw prisoners who had ignored orders to be quiet being swiftly and forcefully carried from the booking area to an isolation cell by three or four deputies.

†Some deputies, if they work in a jail for a long time, get to know some of the jail regulars and interact with them on a broader set of characteristics; and a few prisoners who are known to posssess skills and knowledge that are useful to the jail operation may be dealt with almost as if they were real people. But most prisoners never see this sort of treatment.

the jail, all clothing is taken from the prisoners, and they are supplied with ill-fitting, conspicuous jail uniforms, such as the baggy, bright orange jumpsuits worn by San Francisco County jail pretrial detainees. Most of the other things they use to manage their appearance—the set of tools Goffman refers to as an "identity kit"—are taken from them, and they are allowed to keep only a few (such as a toothbrush, toothpaste, hairbrush, comb, and soap) during incarceration.[6] (In San Francisco and Los Angeles the toothbrush and toothpaste are supplied by the jail, and the other items must be purchased from the canteen.)

It is very often difficult for prisoners to keep clean. A man who had been in several small city and county jails in California told me: "If you wanted to wash you had to wash in the toilet. The whole place was so filthy that I just stayed in my clothes. After a week I got out and took off my shoes. Whew, the smell. I had the worst case of athlete's foot you ever saw. Two toes looked like they were going to fall off." In large, relatively humane county jails, such as those in San Francisco County, prisoners are scheduled to receive a change of clothing about once a week. But to many, this provision has not been reliable or sufficient; the files of the San Francisco jail ombudsman contain complaints like these: "We have not had a clothes change in three weeks. We want a full set of clean clothes once a week." And: "We should be allowed to change underwear twice a week—and have two pairs, so we will not be naked while we wash underwear." Furthermore, it is virtually impossible to be "well groomed" in jail. Shaving is difficult because prisoners are not allowed to keep razor blades, and the deputies usually supply one razor blade a day to be used by many prisoners; in San Francisco, up to twenty prisoners must use one blade for their morning shave. Prisoners have no fingernail clippers. Most jails have no barbers, and prisoners either cut one another's hair with razor blades or let their hair grow.

Although there has been some improvement over the last two decades, the food given to prisoners is often inadequate to maintain health. The usual problems of institutional food (too much starch, too little protein, too bland, too cold) are aggravated by an extremely meager food budget. One prisoner wrote the ombudsman of the San Francisco jails: "There is never enough food on the tray. Also the food is most of the time cold. The amount of food given in this county jail is not enough to feed a five-year-old child." The medical services provided in jails, though better than they once were, are inadequate to deal effectively with many moderate to serious medical problems.[7] Some jails, such as the Los Angeles County jail, have a relatively thorough initial medical screening, but once a prisoner is in the tanks, it is very difficult for him to get treatment for ordinary medical problems. The usual medical routine is a daily visit to the tanks by a medical technician or nurse, who receives complaints and dispenses the common nonprescription medications (aspirin, cold medicines, and laxatives) and gives prescription drugs to particular prisoners. This technician or nurse screens complaints for the physician who usually makes a daily visit to the jail.[8] After a few weeks or months of listening to many trivial or feigned complaints, the technicians and nurses often become skeptical and even cynical, and getting past them to the doctor can be very difficult. As a result, some legitimate medical problems are neglected. As one prisoner wrote in her complaint to the San Francisco County jail ombudsman:

> I sent in three medical requests to see the doctor and I was never called. These were the dates: 10-7-80, 10-15-80, 10-20-80. On the afternoon of 10-27-80 the nurse said I had to send a medical request in. I told her I sent in three. She put in another one. Capt. Y. was nearby, so I told him my problem. Next day I got to see the doctor and she found blood in my urine. I have a history of kidney problems. I had a kidney operation two years ago. I had the same symptoms before the operation as I have now. On the nite of the 11-3-80 I put in another medical request and nothing happened the next day. The morning of 11-4-80 I asked the nurse if I was on the list to see the doctor. She said NO, you are not the only person in this jail that wants to see the doctor and you are not the only one sick. I told her I was passing blood in my urine. She said I don't care. . . .

Most jails make no provision for frequent exercise or outdoor recreation. In San Francisco County, Jail No. 1, where prisoners begin their jail career, has no facilities; No. 2 has a small room in the jail with weights, and prisoners are released to it a few times a week for one or two hours at a time; and No. 3 has a yard to which all the jail's prisoners who are not on restriction are released for two or three hours every clement day. The Los Angeles County jail has a roof to which prisoners are released, on a rotation basis, for several hours a week. In general, it is the exception when a jail prisoner can exercise or be out of doors for more than a few hours a week.[9]

As we have seen, prisoners live in tanks containing crowds of strangers. The human density and total lack of privacy expose them to one another in ways that can occur only in total institutions. They inspect one another's genitals, scars, rashes, and deformities. They smell one another's breath, sweat, gases, and feces. They hear one another's snoring, breaking wind, and masturbating.

Most people depend upon a variety of shields, such as clothing, private rooms, and deodorants, to disguise certain aspects of themselves and to hide their publicly offensive practices. These efforts are more than attempts to "look one's best" or to conform to social standards; they help maintain basic conceptions of self, of individuality. The degradation caused by all jail processes is summed up in the relatively uniform appearance of prisoners—plain, sallow, unclean, disheveled.

Attitudinal Degradation

Many criminal justice functionaries express contempt and hostility toward suspects and defendants, and this fact compounds the degradation experienced by prisoners. This contempt is not idiosyncratic, however. It stems from values shared by police officers, deputies, prosecutors, and many judges. These values are rooted in a theory of crime and society that Herbert Packer has identified as the "crime control model." He writes: "The Crime Control Model is based on the proposition that the repression of criminal conduct is by far the most important function to be performed by the criminal process. The failure of law enforcement to bring criminal conduct under tight control is viewed as leading to the breakdown of public order and thence to the disappearance of an important condition of human freedom."*

The majority of police officers and deputies accept this theory, but they do not see crime control as simply or mainly a practical endeavor. In their view, what threatens the public order is not crime itself but immorality, and the major threat lies in the immorality of certain classes or types of people, most of them belonging to the rabble.

*The Limits of the Criminal Sanction, p. 158. Packer contrasts this model with the due process model, which is dominated by other concerns: seeing that the system does not err in convicting persons of crime, restraining the extension of government power, and ensuring equality of treatment for the defendant.

Arresting officers

The police, who make the initial and highly discretionary arrest decisions, tend to believe that street people or disreputables—the people they arrest most frequently—are the primary source of trouble in society. As Officer C. of the San Francisco police told me in an interview: "It's the people who are hanging around on the corner. They're unemployed and don't have anything else to do. Like the guys on Eighteenth and Mission. They don't act like other people. They don't know when to stop. They're ready to do anything. People who have jobs, live in apartments or houses, they don't cause us any trouble."

Most police officers are not dispassionate toward the rabble. Their personal class prejudices and cultural distaste (to use the mildest term) are strengthened by the irritating and time-consuming task of policing a class of people who have always posed the most visible and offensive problem of social order in big cities.[10] In the neighborhoods where there are significant contingents of the rabble, most police work is directed toward managing them. Officer C. told me: "If you don't keep on top of them, then they get out of hand. If you let too big a crowd of them to form, it will get out of control. They bother people who have to pass them and the business in the area. You have to keep them moving."

Some rabble types consistently show disrespect toward the police and threaten their authority. This failure to show respect often stems from a moral contest between disreputables and police. Most disreputables (as we should expect) operate according to beliefs and values that bolster their dignity and justify their position and behavior as morally correct. These beliefs usually also define police officers as lowly and despicable human beings. So instead of passively or obsequiously submitting to an officer's commands, disreputables may engage the police in a moral contest, objecting and arguing from their own moral position. When police officers who are already hostile toward the rabble are confronted with such hostility and moral condemnation, an invidious dynamic is set in motion. Anything less than complete obedience by the rabble can be seen as a moral or physical threat that must be countered with immediate force.

The hostility of police officers is clearly expressed in the names they use to label the rabble category. Officer C. explained the epithets now in use: "Some guys use slime balls and pukes. I like dirt ball. Now kronks is popular. Assholes is still the most common term." The hostility is also evident in the way police handle disreputable types when they arrest them and take them to jail. Approximately half the persons in our felony sample reported that the arresting officers were verbally abusive to them. For example, "They talked to me like a dog." Or "They talked to me like I was an asshole. I'm not a criminal, I wasn't even high." Seven persons in the sample reported that they were handled in a physically abusive manner. One of them, a twenty-two-year-old Nicaraguan corner boy, said: "I was playing football with my cousin in a field. This cop came up to me with his gun drawn. He pushed me down on the ground. He was shaking. I was petrified. He jerked my hands way up my back and put on the cuffs." In addition, seven others stated that they were struck or kicked by the arresting officers. For example: "They hit me in the face and the stomach when they got me in the car." And this: "He was pushing me in the car and gave me a big kick in the stomach when I was bent over getting in."*

Deputies

Like police officers, jail deputies (employees of the sheriff who run the jail) tend to hold strongly negative attitudes toward most persons who are arrested and held in jail. These attitudes stem largely from their work with prisoners, which is in many ways more annoying than police work. They must constantly handle repulsive, difficult, and even violent prisoners, some of whom are drunk, high, enraged, belligerent, or insane. Many prisoners hate deputies, and a few openly express this hate. For example, I once heard a prisoner who was being booked loudly threaten the booking room deputies as follows: "You rotten motherfuckers, if I catch you on my turf you're in trouble." (The response from one deputy was: "You haven't *got* any turf, asshole.")[11]

*I have only the prisoners' accounts of these acts and do not know what actually happened or what, if anything, had provoked the officers' actions. However, four of the seven prisoners had facial bruises. In his study of police behavior, *The Police and the Public*, Albert Reiss found that in the majority of cases in which the persons arrested were "violent or aggressive" or "disgruntled or sullen," the police used "gross force" or "firm handling, generally moving the offender about by holding him by the arm, prodding him with a nightstick, or surrounding him with several police officers" (p. 54). This suggests that the expression of hostility is interactive. Nevertheless—and this is what is important for this analysis of degradation—many arrested persons in my sample *believed* that police officers had unnecessarily abused them, physically or verbally, and this made them feel both angry and degraded.

Besides occasionally expressing such hostility, prisoners regularly try to combat their deprivation by beseeching deputies for help. Deputies who do not immediately and emphatically rebuff these entreaties are inundated with pleas. New deputies who have not yet acquired the deputies' culture and may have some sympathy for prisoners are especially vulnerable. Roger Martin, a temporary deputy, described his experience in this way:

> Earlier on the job, the inmates conned me often. I learned this is standard procedure with a new deputy. He usually begins as a relatively nice guy before the jail brutalizes him. The inmates try to take advantage of this, to ask for favors and get the deputy to do things for them. I was gullible enough to be conned at first, but I quickly learned they were taking advantage of me and laughing at me behind my back.[12]

These supplications from prisoners confront deputies with a constant moral dilemma. They must work closely with other humans (prisoners) who are in a state of deprivation and visibly suffering. (If the deputies do not notice, the prisoners will remind them.) If the deputies remain committed to a philosophy of humanity and egalitarianism, or even to a basic sense of fairness, the plight of the needy and the suffering around them will eventually take a heavy toll on their peace of mind and personality organization. To avoid this, most deputies embrace and help sustain the theory that prisoners are worthless and deserve their deprivation. For some, who have operated all their lives on similar concepts (stereotypical thinking or racial prejudice), this is relatively easy. Others, however, must consciously reject more humane and tolerant conceptions of prisoners before they can accept the cynical viewpoint. In most cases they cannot accomplish this without some strain, and this strain and their lingering ambivalence often make them *more* expressive of hate and brutality. As in other situations, the convert is very often the extremist.*

Deputies openly refer to prisoners by derogatory names. As Martin described the practice: "The deputies routinely called the inmates asshole or motherfucker to their faces or just out of their hearing. The

---

*I witnessed this process not only in deputies, some of whom I had known as students before they became deputies, but in myself and my fellow prisoner services caseworkers. We were constantly beseeched for more help than we could deliver, and we had to cope with feelings that we were not doing enough. (One knows he can always do more.) In compensation for these feelings, we began to develop a more cynical view of our work and a more derogatory conception of the prisoner. We used the common term *burnout* to describe this process.

terms were so commonly used that they literally became the inmate's name. . . .They look on Mexicans and Blacks as scum. Spic, greaser, jungle bunny, nigger—the names flow effortlessly from the deputy's lips."[13]

The hostility of deputies is by no means exhausted in name calling. It is also expressed in their routine discretionary decisions: whether to allow entering prisoners to make phone calls, or to keep some items on their person, or to eat, or to retrieve money taken from them during arrest. For example, I once asked a deputy who was temporarily in charge of the property room if he could transfer a prisoner's money to his "books" so he could spend it in jail. His answer was: "Fuck the asshole. If it was up to me the assholes wouldn't get anything. If they want to spend their money, let 'em stay out of jail." It is expressed in their decisions to ignore prisoners' visible medical needs; to punish them on the spot for talking, shouting, talking back, or having a "bad attitude"; to place them in cells or tanks where they will be in danger from other prisoners; to keep them locked in cells; to withhold their mail or money sent to them through the mail; to ransack their cells in cell searches; and to subject them to humiliating and painful experiences. An example of one such experience, the "kiester search," is given by Martin:

> "Now bend over and spread your cheeks," I ordered. The kid bent over and grabbed his buttocks, pulling them apart. The plastic bag [of narcotics] inserted into his rectum had broken. The red pills had partially melted from his body heat, and his anus was a flaming scarlet color. The intestinal pressure had forced some of the pills out through his sphincter where they remained matted in his anal hair. We began to laugh with black humor at the grotesque sight. When the cops became bored with the game, the kid was ordered to dig the narcotics out of his rectum.[14]

Sometimes special events or processes inhibit the strong tendencies of deputies to develop or express malevolent attitudes. For example, several court actions apparently have restrained deputies in Los Angeles. Many prisoners and ex-prisoners have reported to me that during the middle 1970s at the Los Angeles County jail deputies became exceptionally abusive to prisoners. One of them said: "Man, someone should do something about that jail. I mean those cops will get on people for nothing. A guy doesn't have to get out of line to get mistreated there. I watched it many times. Young guys who didn't know what was happening, and the cops would yank them out of line and treat 'em like dogs. It made me sick. I haven't seen anything like it in all my years of being in these places." Prisoners at the jail in 1983 suggested to me that a series of lawsuits and court injunctions against the jail had significantly reduced the verbal and physical abuse. As one of them put it: "Yeah, they used to be bad here, but the courts have been on them, and most of that really rough stuff has stopped."

At the Yolo County jail, the friendlier rural atmosphere and the efforts of a relatively humanitarian jail supervisor, who is able to control his small staff effectively, have apparently prevented the normal deputy culture from developing. As one prisoner put it: "This place is a piece of cake. You should look at Sacramento. There it's mean. This place is a playground. Everyone treats you like a human being."

At the San Francisco County jails two humanitarian sheriffs, Richard Hongisto (1972–1978) and Michael Hennessey (1980 to the present), have systematically promoted a humane approach. They have fired or transferred many deputies who were involved in abusive practices and have hired and promoted persons who demonstrate more humanity and tolerance for prisoners. In spite of these efforts, which are still continuing, many deputies at the San Francisco County jails openly revealed their hatred for prisoners during the time I was observing there. They regularly called the prisoners "assholes" and stubbornly resisted the attempts of outsiders, such as the prisoner services caseworkers, to help them.

Judicial Degradation

As Malcolm Feeley has noted in his study of the New Haven court system, court proceedings are conducted as a *moral* enterprise: "Many observers of the courts have become preoccupied with procedural justice, and have consequently failed to appreciate the intensity of the normative concern which informs the decisions of so many officials in the criminal process."[15] More concretely, this means that prisoners are judged not solely or even primarily for their crimes but rather for their character and that they are often profoundly degraded during their court appearances.

Degradation is built into the court routines, which are planned and executed to dignify reputability (and condemn disreputability). Usually the judge is introduced by the bailiff, who orders those present to stand while the judge whisks in to assume his high station. From his lofty seat, which is the largest and most luxurious in the room, he directs the proceedings with virtually absolute official power—including the power to summarily jail anybody in the room for contempt of court. The bailiff attempts to enforce the rigid code of courtroom decorum, which goes far beyond the rules necessary to maintain order and to speed the court process (men must remove their hats, no one may read a newspaper, and so on). The attorneys, clerks, and bailiff address the court, make requests and motions, and generally perform their roles in a practiced manner that shows respect for the judge.

The appearance and behavior of most defendants come into conflict with the ideal decorum of the court. In general, the courtroom actors fall into two visibly distinct categories: rabble defendants and respectable court functionaries. Although the judge in America has removed his wig, he still dons a robe—one of our society's last sartorial symbols of aristocratic elitism.[16] The bailiff wears a sheriff's uniform, and the clerks wear appropriate white-collar dress. The defense and prosecuting attorneys wear society's standard uniforms of respectability.* The appearance of all but a few defendants stands in sharp contrast to this display. As the novelist John Hersey once described the disreputable and bizarre appearance of defendants in the municipal court in New Haven, Connecticut:

> What faces one sees there!—ravaged, jaunty, dazed, disenchanted, raging, resigned. A man in his forties (found intoxicated) clutching in his arms a stuffed tiger nearly as tall as he, his constant companion and only comfort; a natty type accused of gambling, in a whipcord bush jacket and knickers and smartly polished leather puttees; three weedlike red-eyed minors in blue jeans, accused of armed robbery; a woman booked as a whore, with a pokey-soiled wig and a hacking cough, badly in need of night's more merciful light; an empty-faced teenager, held for possession, with his mother, who is played out to the very end of her kitchen string, on hand to stand up with him. . . . This place is society's open sore.[17]

The rabble, marginal rabble, and working-class and lower-class defendants fail to wear a "proper" court uniform. Those who come from the jail usually wear jumpsuits or the clothes they were arrested in—

*There are clear differences in the clothing styles adopted by the prosecution and the defense. Male prosecutors favor conservative three-piece suits and even more conservative shoes—wingtip, plain, or cap-toe brogans. Female prosecutors wear business suits or dresses. Male defense counsels lean toward sportier, trendier, or older suits (corduroy suits and jackets are common) or a sport coat and slacks; they tend to wear moccasins, loafers, or ankle-high boots. Female defense counsels, particularly public defenders, often wear pants or a skirt and blouse.

typically denim pants, T-shirts, and nylon jackets that are worn, torn, and dirty. Those who are out on bail or OR may have tried to "dress up." Some of them wear "hip" street clothes: polyester slacks that are tight at the hips and flared at the bottom, leather jackets, sport shirts with huge collars, high boots, no ties. Others appear in their work clothes or street clothes: cotton pants, open-collared shirts or T-shirts, and nylon jackets. Even the few who appear in coat and tie fail to approximate the style approved by conservative middle-class convention.

Besides appearing out of place, most defendants fail to perform properly and skillfully, and they often disturb or disrupt the routine. When they approach the bench to take their position behind "the bar," some of them meander awkwardly forward with small unsteady steps, hands groping for some comfortable position, head lowered. Others stride forward in an arrogant street gait, arms swinging, body swaying, and head bobbing. Whereas the attorneys are at ease and poised before the bench, most defendants bend and slant their bodies, shift their weight from one foot to the other, fiddle with their hands or perhaps stick them into their front or back pockets. When they sit at the defense table, they slouch and fidget in their seats, jut their legs far out in front of them, and appear to be either too ill-at-ease or too relaxed.

During the hearings many of them fail to respond to the judge's commands or to understand essential information. The more aggressive defendants occasionally pierce the courtroom decorum with disruptive commands, requests, and opinions. Thus, for example, a young man accused of grabbing a radio from another man on the street and then knocking him down—a robbery—loudly protested against his attorney's request to be removed from the case, which would result in a delay: "I've already been here forty-one days and I want to go out and get to work. My birthday is January 26, I sure don't want to be in jail for my birthday." And another defendant argued with the judge over his attorney's motion to have him ruled incompetent. Defendant (loudly): "Certainly I'm competent!" Judge: "Your attorney is not in agreement with you." Defendant (shouting): "How could my attorney not be in agreement with me? He's supposed to defend me. What's crazy about wanting to get out of jail!"

Such behavior by poorly dressed defendants, besides being personally offensive, serves to remind the judge and his court of the importance of observing social proprieties and respecting society's status systems. In a sense, the court is a microcosm and a symbol of society's formal and stratified aspects. The behavior of defendants here is taken as a demonstration of their general social weaknesses and as evidence that they are truly *moral inferiors*. Thus, the court functionaries—particularly the prosecutor and the judge, but also the bailiff, the court reporter, and even the defense counsel—openly or indirectly display their contempt for most defendants, who are thereby humiliated and degraded.

The prosecutor is the most moralistic courtroom actor and the most overt in displaying contempt. The job tends to attract more morally conservative attorneys, and the work itself promotes moral conservatism. The prosecutor's job is to convict. He is rewarded for a high conviction rate and is criticized, even punished, for losing important cases.* To win a conviction, he must pick out and emphasize the most incriminating and blameworthy bits of information; he must characterize the defendant as both guilty *and* reprehensible. It helps his case and also his conscience to believe strongly that the defendant is guilty, morally contemptible, and deserving of punishment. These attitudes appear in all his arguments: the court should rule on a felony charge rather than a misdemeanor, it should set high bail, it should not release the defendant on OR, it should deliver a harsh sentence. Such attitudes even result in openly vindictive actions, such as having persons recharged in the courtroom (sometimes over the judge's objection) with a different but related crime after the original charge has been dismissed. This tactic, when successful, forces the defendant to return to jail and again qualify for bail or OR, even though he has not committed a new crime, and it is legally possible to have him appear on the new charge without being rearrested and booked. (During my observations, I saw this happen several times.)

Judges, in the words of Anthony Amsterdam, are also "solidly massed" against the criminal suspect:

*John Kaplan, a former assistant U.S. attorney, has commented as follows on the awards and criticisms related to winning or losing prosecutions:

> If the assistant making the decision expected to try the case himself, his previous record—often a matter of status within the office—would be at stake. And if he both authorized and tried a losing case, it would be hard for him to contend that he did not make an error in one action or the other. . . . The criticism or, more usually, unwelcome sympathy, produced by the loss of a case was generally far in excess of the congratulations produced by a winning one. (John Kaplan and Jerome Skolnick, *Criminal Justice*, p. 282)

Let there be no mistake about it, to a mind-staggering extent—to an extent that conservatives and liberals alike who are not criminal trial lawyers simply cannot conceive—the entire system of criminal justice below the level of the Supreme Court of the United States is solidly massed against the criminal suspect. Only a few appellate judges can throw off the fetters of their middle-class backgrounds—the dimly remembered, friendly face of the school-crossing guard, their fear of a crowd of "toughs," their attitudes engendered as lawyers before their elevation to the bench, by years of service as prosecutors or as private lawyers for honest, respectable business clients— and identify with the criminal suspect instead of the policeman or with the putative victim of the suspect's theft, mugging, rape or murder.[18]

This lack of sympathy is not restricted to the accused mugger, rapist, and murderer. Judges are also repulsed and angered by the petty criminal and the merely disreputable person. Judges, after all, are symbols of the dignity of the court, even though the modern court cannot always conduct itself in a fully dignified fashion (often because of the presence of disreputable persons). Most of the time, judges who are prejudiced against the parade of disreputable persons who pass through their court manage to disguise their contempt (rather thinly) with an officious and condescending tone. For example, I heard a judge subtly impugn the character of a defendant who had persistently requested a different public defender. Judge: "Does C. have a rap sheet [a record]?" D.A.: "Yes, your honor, an extensive one." Judge: "That explains it." But the prejudice sometimes breaks into the open, as in the following judge's condemnation: "The law gives me no choice but to acquit you. Personally, though, I hope you get hit by a truck as you leave the court."[19]

Most defendants in urban jurisdictions are represented by public defenders or by the court "regulars" who are appointed by the court and paid at fees set by the county. These attorneys lack the time, the inclination, or the resources to prevent a case from being handled in the routine fashion, that is, as a moral issue rather than a due process question. They accept an inverted version of the moral viewpoint of the prosecutor and attempt to help their clients by seeking the court's mercy. They see their clients as guilty but as much less blameworthy. They try to characterize them as victims of hard circumstances, such as poverty and racism, and often argue that their acts are the understandable outcomes of these circumstances or of activities that should not be illegal, such as the use of marijuana.

Acceptance of this inverted version of the moral viewpoint leads these defense counsels to depart from a true adversary position. It makes them more willing to settle their cases through informal negotiation and more willing to operate according to undignified (though sympathetic) conceptions of the defendant. They often reveal these conceptions in their informal interaction with their clients. For example, they usually give the defendant advice on how to dress and act in court. In doing this, they imply not only that the defendant's normal habits are unacceptable (and by implication, that the defendant himself is socially unacceptable), but also that he ought to play his "proper" role in the moral process—that of a diffident, contrite moral inferior.

Loss of Commitment

One basic premise behind the practice of law enforcement as a moral enterprise is the idea that persons will respond to contempt and castigation with apology, contrition, and alteration of their character and conduct. The tenacity of this belief is peculiar in the face of so much contradictory evidence. Under some conditions, of course, some defendants bow and conform when they are degraded, condemned, and disciplined. But under other conditions, which are just as common if not more so, they squirm away from the disapprobation, avoid the punishment, and refuse to follow prescriptions for future conduct. Such conditions are not hard to imagine. The disapprobation meted out to them may be severe, contemptuous, and unmitigated by any positive attitudes. Realistically, there may be no clear paths to their "rehabilitation," that is, to their achievement of dignified social status and economic self-sufficiency. And they may have contact with the deviant viewpoints that characterize the official deliverers of disapprobation and punishment as morally inferior and the "offender" as honorable.

When these conditions apply, many marginal persons lose or relax their commitment to conventional society. This is more understandable when we consider the tremendous effort it can take to maintain that commitment when one is poor and of low social status. It means struggling to meet all the obligations required of a conventional citizen, such as paying rent, bills, taxes, fines, fees, alimony, and child support. It means avoiding deviant habits, such as stealing or excessive drinking and drug use. And it means observing society's pervasive and subtle definitions of respectability, which define in rather narrow terms just how to comport oneself in public. To many persons, the prospect of giving up this struggle looks appealing.

Rejection of conventional values and loss of commitment to society are even more likely to occur when defendants believe that those who punish them in the name of the law are hypocritical and unfair. Due process values—such as "all persons are innocent until proven guilty" and "every person has the right to a fair and impartial trial"—are widely and proudly celebrated in conventional society and often ceremoniously repeated during the judicial process. Yet what the defendants actually experience are the practices that stem from law enforcement conceived as a moral enterprise, practices that involve systematic violations of due process values. Moreover, they believe that they are being intentionally punished during all stages of the judicial process, regardless of its eventual outcome. And in this, they are correct.[20] The great majority of persons arrested do not receive jail or prison sentences; but all of them, including many whose charges are dismissed, are subjected to some punishment. The experience of harsh and unfairly delivered punishment frequently enrages or embitters defendants and makes it easier for them to reject the values of those who have dealt with them in this way.

With their commitment to conventional values damaged or destroyed and their ties to the dominant culture shaken loose, many persons—particularly those who are already living on the margins of conventional society and having difficulty conforming—"drop out": they migrate to deviant worlds and the rabble status. The jail experience prepares them for an acceptance of the rabble life.

6

Preparation

WHILE SERVING as a social institution for controlling the rabble, the jail also supports and maintains the rabble class. For the rabble, it is a meeting house, a place where they find new friends and reconnect with old ones who share common goals and interests. It is a convalescent center, a place where the ailing and tired among them can rest, heal, and ready themselves for another effort at living outside. It is a place where those among them who were migrating back toward a conventional lifestyle are reoriented and reattached to the rabble life. And it is a place where persons already living on the margins of society are introduced to the rabble life and are prepared for the rabble existence. This preparation—which consists of experiences that cannot be avoided—is psychological, cultural, and social.

Psychological Preparation

Losing conventional sensibilities

The preparation for the rabble existence, which is complex and thorough, begins when new prisoners are ushered across an important psychological barrier. Most outsiders see rabble existence as sordid, chaotic, hard, impoverished, and dangerous; and even if they have been close to rabble life, they understand and sometimes share the intense contempt that most people feel toward the rabble. Indeed, the repelling image of the rabble life provides a motivation for many persons, and especially for those who are already struggling to maintain their repute and conventional status. It looms as a warning to them that if they relax their efforts, they may quickly slip into that life.

In the jail experience, many of the repulsive and feared aspects of the rabble life are concentrated into a small space and a short time. It was emphasized earlier that the prisoners unfamiliar with jail were shocked and disorganized by their introduction to it. But as hours or days pass, the shock wears off, and they begin to adjust, even to discover that the jail is not as sordid or threatening as it first seemed. They learn that with some new skills, they can cope with many of the imposed restrictions. For example, they learn how to keep themselves clean, even in these adverse circumstances: "When I first watched guys washing some of their clothes in the toilet I couldn't believe it. Then I saw that they kept the toilet spotless. It began to make sense. After a while I had a whole different attitude toward the toilet."

Similarly, persons who at first feel threatened by the appearance of the disreputable types who fill the tanks slowly become acquainted with some of them. They begin to develop an appreciation for them as individuals with distinct personalities and life histories. They begin to see them as fellow human beings with motivations that are understandable if not attractive.[1] Even if this does not result in affection and friendship, it provides a better sense of predictability and reduces revulsion and fear. The novice learns that he can survive and even circulate among the rabble with some ease.

Interaction and appreciation produce another result: the novice discovers that the condemned, disreputable types have internal defenses for deflecting society's disapproval.[2] These defenses may be individual or collective. In the individual defense, the condemned person usually accepts one of society's general negative stereotypes but claims that it doesn't apply to him. He rationalizes his behavior or makes distinctions between himself and other deviants. For example, one of the persons in my felony sample, a foreign tourist who was arrested when he tried to cash a forged check in a bank, argued: "I'm not a criminal. I just ran out of money and was desperate. I had to do something to get money to go back home."

But it is the collective systems of justification and defense that are more influential in the jail. In the weaker collective systems, the deviants tend to accept society's condemnation of the deviant type to which they belong, but they excuse their behavior as a member of that type on certain grounds, such as social causes beyond their control.

For instance, skid-row alcoholics attribute their downfall to drinking and then to the hostility of the "unfair" world around them. As Jacqueline Wiseman stated it:

> A third aspect of the Skid Row man's frame of reference is his feeling of powerlessness coupled with his sense of a need for cunning to outwit a hostile and unfair world. Economically and socially impotent, he feels always vulnerable and (by his standards) persistently exploited by merchants, agents of social control, by employers, even by street friends. For this reason, he suspects that his day-to-day struggle for survival will fail except for his own talents at counterexploitation.[3]

In stronger collective systems of deviant belief, the deviants define themselves and their lifestyles as superior and conventional people as "squares" or "lames" who follow dull, routinized, and perhaps subservient lives.[4] Prolonged interaction with the jail's disreputables familiarizes the novice with these self-justifying viewpoints and further weakens the psychological barrier to an acceptance of the rabble life.

Acquiring the rabble mentality

Living in the tanks with prisoners who have experienced both jail life and the rabble life also helps the novice acquire the mentality or outlook needed for rabble existence.* First, he learns the rabble *wariness*. As Gerald Suttles points out, in the slums or skid rows where the rabble circulate, the conventional standards for ordering public life do not obtain, and the residents must rely on special systems of order: they restrict their interaction to a few persons with whom they are familiar, and they rely heavily on knowledge acquired by close inquiry into personal character and past history.[5] So it is in the jail. Prisoners, unlike reputable people, do not begin to deal with each other from a position of trust. They begin with wariness.

Seasoned prisoners are constantly wary not only of new prisoners but of dangerous situations, such as an argument that might flare into violence. As one jail veteran told me: "You start off not trusting anybody, at first. Some types, you really don't trust. For instance if you're white, you don't trust black guys. You may get to know a black

*By "mentality or outlook" I mean broad collective patterns of thinking that are taken for granted. Later in this chapter I shall deal with "subcultural orientations," which consist of the more explicit definitions that exist in the world of shared meanings that is carried and conveyed in informal talk.

guy and trust him more. But not at first. But it is more than people. You learn when it's safe to sit down, or when you better keep standing, ready to move."

Prisoners also learn to be wary of "the man" (or the "cops," meaning both jail guards and policemen). They try to be constantly aware of the presence or whereabouts of deputies. (In the Los Angeles County jail, whenever a deputy leaves his station at the end of the module and walks down the glassed-in walkway dividing two sides of a module of cells, the prisoners call out: "Man walking.") Such vigilance is essential to many prisoners who regularly pursue activities that violate the rules, such as smuggling food or gambling for money or cigarettes. But wariness of "the man" is pervasive, and all prisoners tend to develop it.

In addition to being wary, seasoned prisoners are highly *opportunistic*. In their state of deprivation they are constantly alert to opportunities for personal gain. For example, they watch for any chance to "appropriate" useful material—money, food, reading material, paper, pencils, envelopes, cigarettes, or raw material for making prisoner artifacts (such as electrical cords for making "stingers" to heat water). This attitude becomes second nature, and the impulse to appropriate anything that is not carefully guarded carries over to life on the outside.*

The opportunistic attitude also means that prisoners keep an eye out for a chance to exploit other prisoners or jail employees. This exploitation may be as benign as seeking information from a prisoner who has special knowledge or attempting to get a great deal of help from a prisoner services caseworker. But it can also be predatory, as in sexual exploitation (discussed in Chapter 3). Persons who are around prisoners or ex-prisoners a great deal sense this purely opportunistic aspect

---

*The verb *appropriate* describes their attitude better than *steal*. They believe that much of the material they take does not belong to anyone in particular or is being unfairly hoarded and kept from them; they see it as there for the taking. Thus, from a prisoner's point of view, taking food from a jail kitchen is not stealing from the county; it is simply appropriating something. This habit of appropriating translates to an impulse to shoplift after they are released. In jail they are keyed up to and practiced at taking any material that is not carefully watched. When they first get out and circulate around stores where there are thousands of tempting items lying around, apparently not being watched at all, they often, sometimes on impulse, steal things, even when they have money and had not planned to steal anything when they entered the store. This type of incident has been reported to me many times, in several of which the persons were arrested for shoplifting.

of their behavior and come to resent the prisoners as unscrupulous con-nivers. What they fail to appreciate fully are the circumstances that fostered this opportunism and made it useful.

Another facet of the rabble mentality is a spirit of *making do*, which is a part of jail stoicism. Many prisoners take pride in their ability to endure the harsh circumstances of incarceration, expressing it in state-ments such as "I can do this six months sitting on the toilet." They find support in a body of knowledge about the skills needed to avoid doing "hard time"—refusing to accept or adapt to the situation. As Spradley has written:

> The man who has not spent much time in jail finds that it takes a great deal of energy to control himself and appear to be a passive, retiring individual. In a sense, he does hard time while trying to do easy time until he has mastered a passive response to life in jail. One long-time inmate observed: "The guy who you don't notice is really pulling hard time. He holds himself back to keep from causing himself more trou-ble." With each repeated incarceration a man learns a little more fully how to conform and accommodate to the demands of a life in the bucket and thus do easy time. Passivity, in a sense, becomes part of his essen-tial character, an automatic response, one which he no longer has to consciously control.[6]

To a great extent, enduring the adversities of jail prepares persons to deal with the hardships of the rabble existence. After some time in jail, the impoverishment and hardness of the rabble life are not so threatening.

Another part of making do is a spirit of improvisation. Besides ap-propriating things, prisoners replace or manufacture useful articles from any available material. An ex-prisoner at Santa Rita, the Ala-meda County jail, told me:

> They take two [metal] spoons and put a piece of plastic they get from cheese packages between them and wrap the ends of electrical cord around the ends of the spoons. This is a pretty good stinger, but it blows the fuses pretty often. You should see the tattoo needles they make. They take a little electrical motor from some toy or something, attach it to a couple of needles and they have a motorized tattoo needle. They make ink from soot. They burn checkers for the soot. Or they grind up colored pencil leads.

Another former prisoner at the old downtown Los Angeles County jail reported:

> Joe was in the jail over a year fighting an appeal, and he set up a store. He got all the guys with no money to buy the limit of any food we could buy, and he'd give them a small percent of it. Like he would give them enough money to buy a pie and then give them one slice of a pie. Then when everyone else ate theirs, he would have several pies to sell, at a higher rate. But he also made a lot of food. They would sell peanuts on the candy cart, and he'd take a lot of bags of them and mash them until he had peanut butter. And then he'd buy bread from some of the prisoners who didn't have any money and make peanut butter sandwiches to sell. He also bought milk from the cart and soured it, put it in a cloth bag he'd made, let it drain for a couple of days, and ended up with something that was halfway between cream cheese and cottage cheese. His products were a nice break in the lousy jail food.

Like wariness and opportunism, the attitudes, skills, and knowledge related to making do prepare a jail prisoner for the rabble existence.

Finally, the rabble mentality includes a streak of defiance toward conventional society and its agents and in particular toward the agents who figure so prominently in the lives of disreputable persons: police officers, jail deputies, and court functionaries.[7] In the jail, the differences between those who represent society and those who represent the rabble are dramatically apparent. And the jail is where the differences in power are most clearly acted out: it is where agents of conventional society can degrade the rabble and treat them more inhumanely than anywhere else. But because they are human, prisoners are not inclined to endure this treatment passively or complacently (as low-ranking military personnel usually do). Most become embittered by it and begin to defy the other side in one way or another.

This defiant streak is embedded in a set of values that forms part of the general deviant subculture shared by many prisoners. Prisoners come from a variety of deviant worlds, but in jail all of them participate to some extent in one of them—the prisoner world, whose amalgamated deviant belief system is drawn from all the others. The opposition values of jail culture revolve around the central idea that the prisoner has been receiving a "raw deal." He may have received the raw deal at various times: when he was growing up, from his parents or perhaps his school; when he tried to make a living but the government drafted him and made him fight in a war; or when the police harassed him or arrested him and threw him in jail. In his study of a medium-sized Midwestern jail, David Rottman provides evidence that the concept of a raw deal is an important part of prisoner culture: "Everyone in jail has his own hard luck story and personal complaints about the 'raw deal' he received. This common feeling of victimization and similarity of treatment received from the legal process is another factor contributing to the development of the inmate culture."[8]

From this central root, the beliefs and values of prisoners branch off in several directions. Some of these beliefs justify deviant identities and deviant lifestyles and denounce conventional society. Some of them define deviant roles and routines for living that offer a modicum of dignity in the most relevant contexts—jail, prison, and "the streets." The most rapacious set of beliefs defines life as a dog-eat-dog confrontation, from which only the strong and the violent survive. It is this outlook that characterizes a type of prisoner hero, the outlaw, that is becoming more prevalent.

Cultural Preparation

Persons who stay in jail for any length of time will be introduced to and influenced by the jail culture and some of its component deviant subcultures, such as those of the petty hustler, the junkie, the derelict, the outlaw, or the lowrider. This is unavoidable because several characteristics of the tank setting intensify the processes of acculturation.

The first of these characteristics is that prisoners in a tank commingle most of the day and the evening with nothing important to distract or involve them; this leaves them lots of time for talk. Before we consider what they talk about, it will be useful to describe briefly the daily routine in the jail.

The tank's life begins early in the morning, about 6 A.M. when deputies turn on the lights, blow a whistle, ring a bell, or shout a command to rise. The morning meal is brought to the tanks on carts and served to the prisoners in the tank. After the meal prisoners return to their cells, the deputy counts them, and trusties sweep and mop the tank floor. The cells are left open until the next count, meal, and tank cleanup. After lunch there are several more hours when the cells are not locked. This routine is repeated at dinner time, which is again followed by an evening period of unlocked cells.

A few activities punctuate the long periods of idleness. Twice a day on weekday mornings deputies "call a court line," and prisoners with scheduled appearances leave the tank to change clothes and be delivered to court. During visiting hours a deputy occasionally calls one or a few prisoners to meet their visitors. Irregularly, but usually in the late afternoon or early evening, a few attorneys summon their clients to special rooms for consultation. Once a day a nurse or medical technician appears at the front of the tank to receive medical complaints and dispense the common medications: aspirins, cold medicines, and laxatives (constipation is endemic in jails). And, periodically, throughout the day and the night, fish carrying bedrolls appear in front of the tank, waiting for the deputy to let them in and for someone to direct them to a vacant cell and bunk. Balancing this steady influx, deputies sporadically call out a name or two and the order to "roll 'em up" (the bedrolls), which means that those called are leaving the tank (to be released or transferred). On some weekdays the canteen wagon arrives and delivers or sells cigarettes, candy, peanut butter, crackers, soft drinks, toilet articles, stamps, paper, and envelopes. If the jail has a recreation area, prisoners from one or more tanks are released to it for an hour or two once or twice a week, for exercise, games, or just a break from the tank.

During the day shift, into which most of these activities are compressed (mainly for administrative convenience and economy), the jail is busy and noisy. Its cement and metal refract sound, and the clanging, talking, and shouting bounce around and mix together into a steady, dull roar—a frightening sound to those unaccustomed to it. In the evening and on weekends, the pace slows. There are no court lines, no canteen, few releases, fewer visits from attorneys, and virtually no transfers. The staff is reduced, movement about the jail is diminished, and the noise level drops.

This schedule leaves the prisoner with nothing particular to do during most of his waking hours. Passing this time is the most pressing problem of living in the tanks, particularly the pretrial tanks. As one prisoner interviewed by Spradley put it: "Time seems to never end. The day seems forever. You do it one day at a time."[9]

A few of the more depressed or passive prisoners will spend much of their time withdrawing into themselves—sitting, moping, and sleeping. But most prisoners try to entertain themselves during their waking hours. Television watching is common, particularly in the evening, and reading is also popular, although the supply of reading material is quite limited.[10] But talking—or more specifically, "rapping" and "tripping"—is the major way to pass time. As Rottman has put it: "The inmate's day is spent in almost constant conversation, often over cards. In the course of these talkathons, [the inmates] learn a great deal about each other, and this becomes part of the pool of knowledge held by the general subculture."[11]

A second characteristic that promotes acculturation into deviant subcultures is that the talk in a jail tank tends to be dominated by persons who are the carriers of deviant values and beliefs. This is because those in the two highest levels of the tank's social stratification system—the ex-convicts and the petty criminals—are also the dominant public speakers.

At the top of this system are the tank's ex-convicts, men who have served terms in prison. Although they may be outnumbered, they have the edge on other prisoners because of their special knowledge and skills. They can adjust to the jail with less discomfort and more skill than other prisoners. They are much more likely to be acquainted with other prisoners in the jail, to meet persons with whom they "did time" at a prison, or to meet persons with mutual friends in a prison. At the minimum, they all share a special set of cultural traits, a special body of knowledge related to prisons, and a unique identification—that of the ex-convict. Most ex-convicts feel an affinity for one another (except for those who are prison pariahs—snitches, punks, and rapos). This affinity stretches across the many differences that separate convicts in the prison setting—differences in regional and criminal identities and even racial differences.* Partly because they define the jail period as temporary, the ex-convicts make a collective effort to keep the peace; they are usually able to dominate the tank, mediate most hostilities, or arrange for the removal of troublemakers.

Just below the ex-convicts in the power hierarchy of the tank are the petty criminals (usually petty hustlers in the classification system described in Chapter 2)—those charged with petty theft, minor burglaries (stealing from a car), drug possession, and simple assault. They

*In a jail felony tank, a white ex-convict trusty admitted to me that he got along with the black ex-convicts despite the fact that in prison he had been a member of the "Aryan Brotherhood," a group of white racists. When I asked him about racial conflict in jail, he said: "No, none of that shit goes on here. Everyone is involved in his case. When I get back to Quentin, I go right to Max B [the segregated area for prison gangs], but here we're all just convicts."

often serve sentences in the county jail but avoid prison. Many of them know one another from circulating in the same areas in the city (the Tenderloin and the South of Market skid row), from cooperating in criminal activities, or from having been in jail together before. Like the ex-convicts, they are familiar with the jail and form alliances with each other. They do not share the ex-convicts' prison background, and so the ex-convicts feel no strong affinity toward them. But the two groups coexist in peace and participate vigorously in the tank's public activities, particularly its conversations.

The rest of the prisoners in the tank are dominated by the others and are relegated to an inferior status. For the most part, they listen. Exceptions are made for certain youngsters (usually corner boys or low-riders) who may have no previous experience with the jail but come from urban ghettos, slums, or barrios where they have participated in considerable delinquent behavior, such as fighting, stealing, and using drugs. This social background and their youth—with its perceived potentialities of strength, energy, and volatility—can bring them respect; but in order to gain respect they must be diffident toward the elders. If they respect the tank leaders and "don't cause trouble," they are well treated; they may even be befriended by the ex-convicts and permitted to participate in public discourse. This is not to suggest, however, that violence-prone youngsters always respect their elders while in jail. Increasingly, small groups of them not only challenge the authority of older convicts but harass, rob, and assault other prisoners.*

A third special characteristic of the tank setting that intensifies the acculturation process is a certain quality of the talk that dominates: by

---

*For example, consider this report on the work of a black street gang that organized in one of the tanks in Los Angeles:

Clifford Spears . . . had been reassigned to a cell in a row of 26 cells reserved for inmates who were labeled assault risks. The row was controlled by a street gang called the Crips . . . [who had decided] the day before to extort $5 a week from any non-Crips members assigned to the row. Spears, 24, had only a month left to run on a six-month sentence for petty theft and battery. He was a physically large man, and he wanted only to be left alone. That's what he told a Crips gang member who approached him within minutes of his arrival on the tier. "Sodbuster," the gang member yelled, invoking a term used for non-members. Then the gang member struck Spears in the face with his fist.

Spears was killed in the beating that lasted for ten to twenty minutes undetected by the deputy stationed in the glass walkway running along the row. The fifteen prisoners charged with the murder were between the ages of eighteen and twenty-four. See Ted Rohrlich, "Jail Inmate Dies While Rules Hold Guard 'Prisoner,'" p. 1.

and large, it is highly theoretical or removed from reality. Persons are "tripping" or "jiving" about things they did or are going to do on the outside; but because they are not outside but in jail, they are not restrained by direct reality testing. ("Jiving" and "bullshitting" can mean either ideal talk or creative lying.) They can indulge in exaggeration, distortion, and near-fantasy. In fact, they are rewarded for this because it makes their storytelling more powerful and entertaining. In a sense, this activity delivers the folklore and oral histories of the various deviant groups and thus sustains and spreads their subcultures.

Three topics, each of central concern in rabble life, dominate conversation in the tank. The first is street life. The jail, after all, is close to the streets. In prison, the outside world fades away, but in jail it is just outside; persons arrive from and leave for the streets every hour. The kind of street life that commands interest is life in the demimonde. The conversations are accounts of idealized deviant behavior, fabricated renditions of exploits in the realms of sex, drugs, and crime. During his first jail experience, Malcolm Braly, an ex-convict writer, listened to an older thief talk about his safecracking exploits:

> I was in the Frisco City Jail for suspicion of burglary and I fell in, walking and talking, with an older man and his younger partner. They seemed smart and they acted like sober and seasoned thieves working their way through a piece of modest trouble. The older man, call him Bill, floating somewhere in his fifties, liked to talk safecracking, at which, he was willing to admit, he was an ace, and I was pleased to listen as he lectured on such refinements as day com [a situation in which a safe has been left so that it can be opened by turning the combination dial one or two points to the left or right]. . . . Through those slow days in jail, I walked away the time with him reliving the years he had spent studying stolen manuals, the nights spent drinking with straight technicians as he slyly picked their brains, the hours of dry practice and the thrill of big scores beautifully taken. It sang to me.[12]

The second major topic of conversation is the courts. In the pretrial felony tanks, everyone is involved in a case. As with the streets, prisoners are constantly going to and coming back from the courts. Besides having his own case on his mind, a prisoner is likely to be concerned with others' cases. The whole judicial process becomes a topic of interest and considerable debate. In these conversations, prisoners build up an interpretation of the judicial system as hypocritical and unjust, and this interpretation becomes an important part of their deviant belief systems.

The third major topic is prisons—the "joints." We have already noted that the tank is dominated by its ex-convicts. In addition, there is some flow back and forth between the jail and the joints, as prisoners leave for prison and convicts return for court appearances. For the ex-convicts and convicts, the prison has a special meaning; they have had common experiences there and perhaps mutual friends or acquaintances as well. Talking about the joint is pleasurable for them. Many persons who have not been to prison listen and ask questions about it, and what they hear serves to prepare them for possible prison experiences in the future. Jail prisoners begin their acculturation for prison in the jail.

The acculturation processes that Edwin Sutherland has codified into a proposed general theory of crime causation operate with more intensity in the jail than in any of the other recognized nurturing grounds for deviance—such as the prison, street corners, or other public hangouts. Briefly stated, Sutherland's "differential association" theory argues that a preponderance of criminal definitions, when intensely delivered by persons with prestige, will teach persons criminality.[13] Although the theory may fall short of being a general theory of crime causation, it certainly identifies a process through which deviant subcultures can be transmitted; and the jail supplies all the conditions necessary for the operation of this process, and then some.

The three topics we have identified, with all their idealized renditions of various aspects of the rabble life, almost totally dominate public discourse in the jail. Novices or the marginal rabble receive more than a preponderance of deviant definitions in this setting. They receive only deviant definitions. Some prisoners in the jail have more conventional viewpoints, but these are invariably withheld, suppressed, or drowned out by deviant ones.

Being completely surrounded by persons who possess deviant viewpoints and who behave in jail according to the values inherent in those viewpoints must inevitably influence the perspective and behavior of anyone who spends much time in jail. As one ex-prisoner said:

> When you go to jail you have to live a twenty-four-hour day with the other inmates. If you want to survive and achieve at least a minimum

degree of comfort you have to learn to adapt to the norms of the majority of the other inmates. The degree to which you become one of them determines how successfully you adapt and for the most part makes your time easier or harder. You can't act the part. For twenty-four hours a day, seven days a week, you have to be an inmate. By the time you are released this role will be a part of you.

Social Preparation

The rabble existence is cooperative. Various rabble types "socialize" together in a variety of hangouts—street corners, bars, restaurants, residences, poolrooms, alleys, or parking lots. Wiseman has described the intense social life on skid row:

> A walk on Skid Row on a passably nice day is different from a walk in almost any other part of the city—even ignoring the obvious physical deterioration of the area. The difference is that social life, which in other areas is usually conducted in homes, restaurants, cars, shops, and other more enclosed spaces, takes place on Skid Row on the sidewalk much as it does for children playing in a suburban cul-de-sac. In other parts of the city, the sidewalk is used by adults as a pathway between a point of origin and a point of destination so that it presents areas of continual, on-going movement. On Skid Row, however, the sidewalks are used as areas for conversing, drinking, watching traffic, and panhandling.[14]

The friendship networks among the rabble are more or less open. In the case of derelicts, they are very open. As a drunk interviewed by Wiseman put it: "Skid Row accepts anyone, I don't care who you are, they'll drink with you."[15] Other disreputable types are somewhat less open to immediate socializing. Being in jail, however, automatically inserts one into many of the rabble networks. It does not matter whether a person has acquaintances or friends among active rabble groups outside or whether they would have accepted his participation in their social activities, such as hanging out on the street; a stay in the jail will put him in contact with them.*

*In a conversation about jails, Laud Humphreys, a professor of sociology who had recently served a sentence in a county jail for burning his draft card, told me that after he was released, he walked through a neighborhood where many of the ex-prisoners live and hang out; many persons recognized him, called out to him, and talked to him. He was surprised, he said, at how friendly they were to him.

Besides socializing, disreputables work together to subsist. To some degree, they cooperate in stealing, hustling, panhandling, and "working the welfare system"; in finding a bed, a hotel room, or place to sleep on the streets; and in obtaining food, wine, drugs, clothing, or transportation. These relationships for "instrumental" activities are often formed in jail:

> We were all freed within a week of each other, and one afternoon not long after I ran into Bill's partner on the street. He was a man who had started life by trying to work, but he had liked drinking and partying too much and had slid out of his community into the streets. He was broke, as I was, and he suggested we try something together. It was reasonable. Who is more likely to be trustworthy than someone you have just met in jail?[16]

Conclusions

The jail is a location where the rabble life is not only controlled but compacted. Consequently, it is the primary socializing institution of the rabble existence. Effective socializing institutions, such as the family and the school, hold people in sustained relationships and provide the settings and the time needed to communicate the norms and meanings of the society. They also invest the carriers of the culture with prestige and power so that they can be effective agents of socialization. This is the case with the jail, except that it socializes persons into deviant or outsider cultures. Therefore, it must have some additional aspects designed to counter the influences of the dominant culture. These it has. As noted in Chapters 3, 4, and 5, many processes in the jail disengage people from the dominant society and embitter them toward it. Also, being in jail reduces the fear and revulsion a prisoner may have felt for the rabble existence and, therefore, removes an important psychological barrier to an acceptance of it. Finally, like most successful socialization institutions, the jail provides novices with ties to a real world—in this case, the deviant world of the rabble.

The conversion to the rabble status is by no means an inevitable consequence of being jailed. Most persons with at least a partial commitment to conventional society probably survive being jailed without excessive or permanent damage to their conventional relationships. In fact, considerable anecdotal data convince me that most persons who are jailed once, or even twice, rebound from the experience and try vigorously, at least for a while, to reestablish their position in conventional society. However, several arrests and several periods in jail make this sort of effort increasingly difficult and the jail's socializing processes increasingly more powerful. Age is probably an important variable here. The young and the old, whose attachments to society may be relatively weaker, are probably more susceptible to the jail's socializing power. Some data support this thesis. Age of first arrest has been one of the consistent correlates of future criminal activity. When Marvin Wolfgang, Terence Thornberry, and Robert Figlio examined the arrest records of every male born in Philadelphia in 1945, they discovered that the probability of a person in the "birth cohort" being rearrested after being arrested one or more times was small and did not change a great deal until the fifth arrest, after which the probability rose dramatically.[17] The popular interpretation of this finding is that the small group from the cohort who went on to more than five arrests were "recidivistic" criminals from the start. An equally persuasive interpretation is that going to jail too many times finally converts persons into committed deviants.

Finally, we should be deeply concerned about the socialization of new outlaws, who are the extreme product of the disintegration, disorientation, degradation, and preparation that takes place in the jail and who fashion their behavior after a model eloquently analyzed by Jack Abbott, an archetypal outlaw: "The model we emulate is a fanatically defiant and alienated individual who cannot imagine what forgiveness is, or mercy or tolerance, because he has no *experience* of such values. His emotions do not know what such values are, but he *imagines* them as so many 'weaknesses' precisely because the unprincipled offender appears to escape punishment through such 'weaknesses' on the part of society."[18] Abbott's own behavior offers a chilling example of what can happen when this model is followed. While serving a life sentence in a Utah state prison, Abbott began writing to Norman Mailer, who then led a successful effort to have him paroled. A few months after being released, Abbott stabbed and killed a waiter in an alley behind a restaurant in Manhattan's East Village. Abbott had asked the waiter where the toilet was and the waiter had told Abbott to follow him outside. Abbott interpreted this as a challenge, and when the waiter turned around to face him, Abbott stabbed him in the chest.

In an interview on national television, after being convicted of this homicide and given another life sentence in prison, Abbott argued that he should have been found not guilty for reasons of self-defense because all his prison training had taught him to interpret the type of behavior the waiter had displayed as an attack and to defend himself by acting in the manner he did.

7

Rabble, Crime, and the Jail

O<small>VER THE YEARS</small>, scholars and critics have made many recommendations for diminishing the worst effects of the jail. They have suggested that a high percentage of the jail's intake population could be eliminated through decriminalization. According to Hans Mattick:

> Decriminalization does not imply social approval of conduct previously defined as criminal. It simply asserts what has become historically evident: that criminal law is not equally effective in dealing with all forms of individual and social deviance, and that it is time to deal with such conduct, insofar as it remains problematic after the criminal stigma has been removed, by more appropriate agencies, e.g., medicine, public health, welfare, and family counseling.[1]

Critics have suggested that many more persons who are arrested could be "diverted" before trial. Edith Flynn notes:

> Early diversion techniques at the arrest and pretrial level appear to be . . . ideally suited to lighten the burden of the jail by keeping socio-medical and morals problem cases out of the criminal justice system. For example, if the police were granted more discretion in handling alleged offenders, public intoxicants and other alcohol-related offenders could be diverted into detoxification or alcoholic-treatment programs.[2]

It has been suggested that by expanding programs for release on one's own recognizance, all but a very few of those not diverted could be released before trial, and it has even been suggested that money bail could be abolished. Writes Ronald Goldfarb:

> The only way to perfect the pretrial system is to abolish money bail completely and to devise an open and careful scheme for determining pretrial release and detention. . . . It should include a clear judicial procedure which would strike a reasonable balance between proper demands for detaining the few defendants who are dangerous and assuring the freedom of the many defendants who are not. . . . Detention should not result from the fact that a defendant cannot afford a bail bond; it should arise only when defendants are demonstrably dangerous.[3]

Some critics have argued that pretrial detainees should be given speedy trials or should be held for trial under very different circumstances: "Persons detained awaiting trial should be entitled to the same rights as those persons admitted to bail or other form of pretrial release except where the nature of confinement requires modification."[4]

Finally, critics have suggested that most defendants who are convicted should not be subjected to the cruel and pernicious practices of our current jails but should be placed in programs designed to improve their life chances after release: "Ideally, jails as we have known them should be eliminated. They should be replaced by a network of newly designed, differently conceived [metropolitan and rural] detention centers."[5]

We cannot be certain that these recommendations would solve all the jail's problems or that they would not produce new ones we cannot foresee.* From a practical point of view, however, this lack of certainty seems almost irrelevant. Reform proposals like these have been made many times during the last twenty years, and yet with few exceptions (usually in small, rural jurisdictions) they have not been implemented, and jails have remained the same or become worse.[6] The reason for this is simple: the public and most criminal justice function-

---

*All these recommendations sidestep a central problem in criminal justice—the misuse of discretionary power. When some, but not all, persons are diverted, released on their own recognizance, or sentenced to "alternatives," the decisions are bound to be influenced by whim and prejudice. This problem was examined at length by the American Friends Service Committee, which produced *Struggle for Justice* (1971), a key document in the literature of modern criminal justice. As one who worked on the report, I am convinced that the misuse of discretionary power is a fundamental issue in jail reform. But to delve into its complexities here would divert attention from what I consider the primary obstacle to reform—the public and government posture toward the rabble.

aries do not want to see the rabble treated any differently from the way they are now.

This attitude was clearly revealed when Goldfarb presented his reform ideas in a court that was hearing a suit against a medium-sized jail outside the city of New Orleans. According to Goldfarb, the defense counsel began to ask him a long line of questions:

> [He inquired] whether I would allow jail inmates to mingle, to partake in unlimited recreation, to have unlimited visits, to work, to cohabit sexually. To each question I responded that I felt jail inmates should be permitted to do all these things and more, since their partaking in such activities need not detract from the ability of jail administrators to assure their presence at trial and to maintain the segregation of dangerous defendants from the free community. Once contained, they should be punished no more. After having led me down this path, the defense counsel, obviously pleased with his ability to push me into what he thought was an obviously untenable position, announced his surprise that an outsider to the local scene, a supposed expert, would make such outlandish, bizarre suggestions recommending practices which he felt would be considered exotic in his community. I was proposing, he said, no more than a kind of hotel for criminals.[7]

Goldfarb defended the reasonableness of his ideas by noting that even a presidential commission had made similar recommendations. But that argument misses the point. Such reform proposals really *are* outlandish and bizarre not because they are unworkable or inconsistent with concepts of justice and humanity, but simply because they are the opposite of what the public wants. The public does not want the rabble confined in a hotel; it wants them to suffer in a jail. In our society, the jail will not change until we significantly reduce the size of the rabble class or significantly change our attitudes toward it. Unfortunately, the existence of both a rabble class and public hostility toward it seems to be firmly rooted in our society.

The Rabble: A Permanent Underclass

The rabble class is a product of many of our basic social processes. It is related to individualistic cultural values that promote estrangement. It is related to the continuing influx of nonwhite immigrants who are occupationally unprepared and vulnerable to discrimination based on strong racial prejudices. It is also related to the "suspended" social status of American youth. Young people are rarely admitted to adult social activities and institutions until they are in their twenties.[8] During this extended period of prohibition they are freed from many adult responsibilities and offered a great deal of leisure time. But they do not spend this time passively, patiently waiting to be admitted to adult status. Instead, they invent their own social worlds. Some of these worlds are bizarre and deviant, and many of them, notably those in which drug use is prominent, recruit members into the rabble class.

Finally, the existence of the rabble class is related to persistent ("structural") unemployment among our least integrated citizens, especially among nonwhite minorities and black youth. Troy Duster, noting the widespread futility and despair caused by this unemployment, suggests that "something 'new' has happened to black youth: both an objective, structural change, and for the first time, the beginnings of an *aggregate, subjective, permanent* consignment" to an urban underclass.*

It appears that our society is not only maintaining its conventional class divisions but is also widening the gap between conventional society and a large underclass, whose members for all intents and purposes are outside the society. Of course, the rabble class may shrink or expand somewhat with changes in the economy, immigration patterns, government policies toward the poor, and shifts in cultural values. In the 1980s—when the change from "smokestack" to "high tech" industries is dislocating large sections of the working class, when there is relatively high unemployment, and when the executive branch of government glorifies self-serving individualism, reduces support for the poor, abandons affirmative action, and adopts tax and revenue policies that increase economic disparities—the rabble class has expanded significantly. But even in periods when things were somewhat better for the poor, as in the 1960s, there was a large rabble population, indicating perhaps that it is a permanent feature of our social and economic structure.[9]

---

*Duster offers some frighteningly impressive evidence. The unemployment rate for black youth between the ages of sixteen and nineteen rose from 12.1 percent in 1960 to 48.3 percent in 1983. In 1979, according to the official statistics of the FBI's *Uniform Crime Reports*, 15 percent of this age group were arrested; in that year the same age group committed 26 percent of all violent juvenile crimes and more than 26 percent of all crimes against property. See Troy Duster, "Social Implications of the 'New' Black Urban Underclass," p. 3.

Hostility Toward the Rabble Class

Negative attitudes toward the rabble are deeply embedded in the American social structure and its social processes. Historically, one primary source of the hostility is a generalized fear among conventional citizens that the rabble class collectively threatens the social order with riots, revolution, or at least corruption. Thus, at the end of the last century, when this fear was stronger, Charles Loring Brace could expect widespread agreement when he wrote: "Let the law lift its hand from [the dangerous classes] for a season, or let the civilizing influences of American life fail to reach them, and, if the opportunity offered, we should see an explosion from this class which might leave this city in ashes and blood."[10] Although the fear of a revolution set off by the rabble class is no longer very strong, many people still believe that the rabble may occasionally explode into riot (as they did in the 1960s) and that they constantly assault the "moral fiber" of society.

Another source of hostility toward the rabble is the deep resentment that conforming individuals harbor toward deviants. In the late 1930s, in his book *Moral Indignation and Middle-Class Psychology*, Svend Ranulf suggested that throughout modern history middle-class persons, especially those from the lower middle class, have pursued the bourgeois virtues of frugality, hard work, and honesty at the expense of their expressive impulses so that they have endured unexciting and unsatisfactory lives. For this reason they have resented those who do not appear to be making the same sacrifices, and they have wanted to punish them for living a life of indulgence.[11] This attitude, which has been described by American writers and artists for well over a century, remains part of our society's dominant culture. With considerable effort, most of us pursue conventional and usually materialistic goals, even though we suspect that they do little to change dull lives. Most of us are repulsed and frightened by the rabble, whom we see as indolent, dissolute, and immoral; and most of us, as Ranulf suggested, want to see them punished.

The appearance and behavior of the rabble, even when perfectly legal, threaten conventional citizens in a more fundamental and personal way. City dwellers manage to live among strangers by obeying the unspoken rules that govern almost every imaginable bit of public behavior. They put on a display of respectability that is composed of dress, speech, and gestures. When they do not recognize the same sort of display in others with whom they must mingle, they become nervous or even fearful because they cannot assume that things will run smoothly; their peace of mind, their dignity, even their lives may be in danger. Erving Goffman, who thoroughly explored this aspect of public order, stated it as follows:

> It is inevitable, then, that citizens must expose themselves both to physical settings over which they have little control and to the very close presence of others over whose selection they have little to say. The settings can bring disease and injury to those in them. And others present can introduce all the basic dangers inherent in copresence: physical attack, sexual molestation, robbery, passage blocking, importunity, and insult.[12]

Members of the rabble incite fear and hostility in conventional people because the rabble regularly violate the rules of public life and display themselves in an outlandish, bizarre, repulsive, or threatening fashion.

Finally, America's perception of "the crime problem" draws hostile attention to the rabble. Many of the patterns listed above (individualism, competitiveness, consumerism, socioeconomic stratification), as well as our tolerance of successful but illegal monetary pursuits, have produced a very high crime rate in the United States. Statistically, rabble crime (or street crime, its rough equivalent) is only one of the problems; and most serious crimes—involving heavy property loss and physical harm or loss of life—are committed by "reputable" people from the middle and upper classes. Nevertheless, it is rabble crime that is most visible, inspires the most fear, and precipitates the most anger.

The police have been instructed by the public to do something about street crime. Because they have been unable to reduce it, no matter what they try, they have responded to the public mood by treating the rabble they arrest as if they were serious felons, though most of their crimes are petty.[13] Some of them, moreover, receive prison terms—the full punishment intended for serious criminals.

Why the Campaign Against the Rabble?

Even though the rabble are not responsible for a great deal of serious crime and even though they receive police attention more because of their disrepute than because of their crimes, the fact remains that they *are* bothersome, they *do* commit some crime, and they *do* inspire a great deal of fear among conventional citizens. Does this justify the long-standing campaign against them, even though the evidence suggests that it has had little impact on crime rates? Two students of the police, James Q. Wilson and George Kelling, conclude that it does; and their opinion should be noted since one of them, Wilson, has been a highly influential defender of conservative views on crime and police work.[14]

In an article about the use of foot patrols in a "dilapidated area in the heart of Newark," Wilson and Kelling admit that the return to this older police method, like other variations in police work, has little real impact on reducing crime. They claim, however, that it does serve to reduce fear by controlling disreputables: "We tend to overlook or forget another source of fear—fear of being bothered by disorderly people. Not violent people, nor, necessarily, criminals, but disreputable or obstreperous or unpredictable people: panhandlers, drunks, addicts, rowdy teenagers, prostitutes, loiterers, the mentally disturbed."[15] Another benefit of the campaign against the rabble, they argue, is that it prevents neighborhoods from deteriorating. Tolerating the rabble is like neglecting broken windows (the title of their article), which leads to all the windows in a building being broken: "We suggest that 'untended' behavior also leads to the breakdown of community controls. A stable neighborhood of families who care for their homes, mind each other's children, and confidently frown on intruders can change, in a few years or *even* a few months, to an inhospitable and frightening jungle."[16]

These justifications ignore several serious problems created by the campaign against the rabble. In the first place, it is undeniable that whim, prejudice, misunderstanding, and corruption influence the decisions about which forms of disreputable behavior and which disreputable persons should be controlled. Race, age, and social class—factors independent of actual behavior—contribute significantly to the assignment of intolerable disrepute. For example, a group of noisy black teenagers on a street corner is much more likely to be perceived as threatening by white citizens and the police than a group of equally loud white teenagers. In a middle-class white neighborhood, a male stranger in scruffy work clothes is much more likely than a well-dressed man to be perceived as disreputable and possibly dangerous, even though one is an honest laborer walking to a garage-cleaning job whereas the other is a swindler selling expensive but worthless house sidings. Race often overrides all other visible qualities in the assignment of disrepute. Thus, a colleague of mine, a black professor at a major university, reports an incident in which he was walking at night down the sidewalk of an almost deserted business street in his college town when he saw a middle-aged white woman approaching. As they drew near, she looked at him and gasped: "Oh my God, is this it?"

The *Los Angeles Times* recently documented how the police often treat respectable black males as disreputables:

> There is a well-established rule of caution in the black community that says: If you are black, any contact with the police can unexpectedly become deadly. To Udell Carroll, what happened to him one night last February best illustrates that fear. Carroll, 36, an insurance salesman, pulled into the driveway of his home near 63rd Street and Crenshaw Boulevard after a brief ride through the neighborhood in search of his 16-year-old son. Carroll thought that the boy was out later than he should be; in fact, the boy was already home. Inside the three-bedroom house, family and friends were chatting amiably. His two youngest children were asleep in the back bedroom. As Carroll got out of the car [in front of his home], he noticed two policemen behind him. Suspecting he was a burglar, they had followed him. They ordered him to put his hands up. Carroll said he was confused but careful not to antagonize them. He said he raised his hands and then asked, "What's this all about?" In the moments that followed, the scene turned violent. Carroll suffered a nasty head wound that required 18 stitches to close. Forced from the house, his family and friends stood shivering in the cold night air as police cars surrounded the house and a helicopter hovered overhead. The children watched in terror as white men in blue uniforms, guns drawn, dragged their father and their 16-year-old brother away in handcuffs. . . .
>
> Roosevelt Dorn, now a Juvenile Court judge in Inglewood, said he was roughed up by two police officers who stopped him during a robbery investigation and did not take the time to ask him why he was carrying a gun. He was a deputy sheriff at the time.
>
> Rep. Mervin Dymally (D–Los Angeles), then a state senator, said he was clubbed at a demonstration by a police officer who the congressman said refused to listen to his attempts to identify himself.
>
> John Brewer, son of Deputy Chief Jesse Brewer, the highest ranking black in the Police Department, was forced to lie spread-eagle on the ground after a traffic stop.
>
> Johnnie L. Cochran, Jr., then an assistant district attorney, said he

was forced out of his car at gunpoint and ordered to put his hands above his head as his two crying children watched fearfully from the back seat. Cochran said the officers told him they stopped him because they believed the Rolls-Royce he was driving was stolen.[17]

In reality, the police, who are given the task of actually controlling disreputables, consistently overextend the public's categories. This happens because the police tend to develop a simplistic view of society in which there are only good guys and "assholes" (or whatever is the currently fashionable police label for unworthy pariah). Joseph Wambaugh, an ex-policeman who has produced an impressive sociology of police work in his books, presents an exaggerated characterization of policemen who hate broad categories of people:

> A Hollywood Boulevard fruit-hustler was lurking around the corner of McCadden Place observing that Tyrannosaurus was alive and well and strolling down the boulevard dressed in blue. He was referring, of course, to the street monster Buckmore Phipps, who was perfectly ecstatic today. The reason for Buckmore Phipps' delight was strolling along beside him; his old partner, Gibson Hand. And the fruit-hustler had only to take one look at *that* bad news nigger to know it was time to go pushin. Actually, Buckmore Phipps never even noticed anymore that Gibson Hand was a nigger. Buckmore Phipps hated all niggers. He also hated greasers, slopeheads, kikes, judges, lawyers, fags, dopers, reporters, politicians in general, Democrats for sure, his brother and sisters, the chief of police, his ex-wife *most* assuredly, and all but a handful of other cops. Gibson Hand was one of the few people he didn't hate. The reason he didn't hate Gibson Hand is that Gibson Hand hated *everybody.*[18]

The tendency to develop hate for increasingly broader categories of people will usually prevail unless it is checked by special processes that are not inherent in police work. In fact, the tendency is promoted when police are encouraged to control categories of disreputables.

Another serious problem with the campaign against the rabble and other disreputables is that it fails. Neighborhoods with concentrations of disreputables, at least in San Francisco, are seldom the "stable neighborhoods of families who care for their homes" that Wilson and Kelling talk of protecting. They are places like the Tenderloin or the South of Market, where dilapidated buildings, long neglected by absentee owners, offer cheap rents and attract only impoverished immigrants, derelicts, petty thieves, hustlers, prostitutes, junkies, hoodlums, crazies, and poor elderly people. Or they are places like the

Mission District and Hayes Valley, where lower-class nonwhite families concentrate. And the rowdies in these neighborhoods are young nonwhite males, over 50 percent of them unemployed, who have little to do but hang out together and watch the affluent society around them, a society they have no hope of joining.

The deviance and petty crime (and even serious crime) that abound in these neighborhoods are uncontrollable by any police campaign short of a Vietnam-style war effort. Knowledgeable and honest policemen admit this. Police Lieutenant Ron Flict tried for several years to rid Hollywood, California, of prostitution, an effort in which he used decoys, foot patrols, horse patrols, and even bicycle patrols. He remarked that prostitution is "like a water balloon. You squeeze it in one place and it squeezes out between your fingers somewhere else."[19] Nor are the crimes committed by persons like Eddie Turner preventable by stepped-up police activity:

Turner, shirtless and muscular, his body tattooed and scarred, joined the group after returning from an unsuccessful morning's search for work. "They say, 'Sorry there are no openin's, but if you take a seat and fill out an application, we will get back to you when there is.' They never do," he said. Because there are so few businesses in Watts—most fled after the riot 17 years ago and never returned—job hunting usually involves going outside the community. Turner's journeys have taken him from Redondo Beach to the Los Angeles factories, fast-food restaurants, and hotels. At least three times a week, he said, he was making a journey in search of work. "I go by bus, my mother's car, sometimes a friend drops me off," he said. "Sometimes it gets frustrating. I feel bad about being rejected. I feel like I'm not accepted; they don't want me. But I can't let one job stop me. If they don't call me back, I can't sweat it. There are jobs out there—I know it. You got to get out and get them. So every day I think about getting a job. . . . I need one real bad." There is another dilemma, a hidden penalty. Because Turner and his two brothers are over 18 and out of school, their mother's welfare check has been cut, even though they continue to rely on her for support. Lucita Turner winds up struggling to raise her four children with money meant for her and her 17-year-old daughter. So Turner's mother pressures him to move out and his need for a job, money, and independence grows, [but he is] stymied by meager qualifications—high school dropout and former street gang member. It was not supposed to be this way. He used to dream of becoming a plumber, carpenter, or mechanic. He wanted to move to the mountains where a teacher once took him to spend a few weeks away from the inner city, and where he vowed to return. For a brief while, his ambitions seemed to have a chance. Turner worked as a plumber's assistant. But he was injured on the job and replaced. Now ambition labors against the lure of "the streets"—alcoholism, welfare, broken homes—and the pull of an underground economy in which a career can be had selling drugs. In the projects, young men openly market "sherms" (cigarettes dipped in PCB) for $20 to $30 a stick. It is an option Turner says he rejects, for now. "It's a jungle," he said. "People killing, stealing, and breaking into your house, 'cause they ain't got no funds. . . . It just ain't right. Everybody's hustlin' and scufflin' for every dime they can get . . . tryin' to figure out what moves they can make to get some money." "They used to break into your house and steal TVs and stereos. Nowadays they break into your house, go to your refrigerator and steal your food, your food stamps. . . . People are hungry. I know, I been there. . . . Everybody likes to get a little place and hide. Most people think it's hopeless . . . there's no way they gonna get a job. . . . Some my friends is dead, some in jail and some doing suicidal things flippin' off on the sherm." . . .

It was eight days ago that Eddie Turner talked about the pain of trying to find a job. It was three days later that Lucita Turner talked about her worst fears, that "the streets" would capture her son. And it was a day later that the streets did just that. Eddie Turner was arrested on suspicion of robbing a man at gunpoint not far from his Jordan Downs apartment. He was jailed in the county's Wayside Honor Rancho in Saugus in lieu of $5,000 bail. He faces at least two years in prison if convicted.[20]

In fact, the campaign against the rabble not only fails. It makes matters worse. Focusing on disrepute blurs the distinction between actual crime and what is merely bothersome or offensive. Although some disreputables do pose a real threat to persons and property, their threat is usually not a serious one. For the most part, they steal or hustle small amounts of money or property, and they rarely inflict serious bodily harm (occasionally a purse-snatching or mugging does result in more serious injury). Wilson and Kelling argue that the skilled foot patrolman makes intelligent distinctions and keeps the merely bothersome or repulsive behavior within acceptable limits and scares off or arrests the persons who are real threats. My study has convinced me otherwise. Police officers consistently overextend the disreputable categories, and they gather up many persons who are merely bothersome or offensive and subject them to the harsh and alienating experiences of arrest, booking, and jail.

Finally, the campaign against the rabble is a political diversion. The public is deeply threatened by serious crime, mildly threatened by petty crime, and bothered by the rabble. The police cannot find many serious criminals, so they go after petty criminals and disreputables. Actually, the campaign against petty criminals and disreputables is a second-order diversion; to a great extent the public fears petty crime because the mass media and politicians have systematically diverted attention away from our most serious crime problems. The "street crimes" that the public fears, in part because they are so heavily publicized—mainly stranger-to-stranger homicides, rapes, and assaults, robberies, and burglaries—are not by any objective measure the country's most serious crimes. In recent decades criminologists have begun to discover that the most serious crimes, measured by loss of money and loss of life, are committed by reputable people whose actions are not usually scrutinized by policing agencies; these people are rarely prosecuted, and they almost never go to jail.

Most persons who study America's crime problem have conceded that the financial cost of the crimes of reputable people is many times greater than the cost of street crime. In their introduction to *Corporate Crime*, Marshal Clinard and Peter Yeager have gathered some of the opinions on its cost:

> According to a *New York Times* (July 15, 1979) survey, "Government experts estimate that violations of antitrust, tax, fraud, bribery, pollution, and other federal laws by the nation's thousand largest corporations cost the economy billions of dollars." A former U.S. Deputy Attorney General stated that the Justice Department does not even know the magnitude of damage done by undetected corporate crimes—the dollar losses or the physical injuries to the public and to employees. The Judiciary Subcommittee on Antitrust and Monopoly, headed by the late Senator Philip Hart, [estimated that] faulty goods, monopolistic practices, and other violations annually cost consumers between $174 billion and $231 billion. A Department of Justice estimate put the total annual loss to taxpayers from reported and unreported violations of federal regulations by corporations at $10 to $20 billion, and the Internal Revenue Service estimated about $1.20 billion goes unreported each year in corporate tax returns.[21]

Reputable people also commit crimes or intentional acts that kill and injure many more people than street crime ever touches. In 1984 there were about 20,000 "traditional" murders in the United States. In the majority of these, the murderer was a friend, spouse, or acquaintance of the victim and was acting in a state of anger or rage. There were less than 8,000 occurrences of murder by a disreputable stranger. Physicians and drug companies are culpable for a much larger share of the nation's deaths than traditional murderers. Physicians continue to dispense drugs that have limited efficacy and present substantial risks to patients, and they recommend and perform surgeries that are unnecessary and result in a high death toll.* We ought to remember, when we think of crime, that more than 100,000 workers die every year from industrial diseases (not to mention industrial accidents, which claim another 15,000 lives). These deaths are not the unavoidable result of occupational risks; they are the result of intentional actions taken by reputable people. Several studies have shown that when medical researchers first identify an occupational disease, such as byssinosis (brown lung) or asbestosis, the industries involved invariably attempt to deny or suppress evidence related to the existence of the disease, its seriousness, or its link with the industry. When the evidence can no longer be denied, the industry successfully lobbies to manipulate the applicable laws or regulations so that it will have to make only minimal changes in its operations—even when there is substantial evidence that those modified operations will continue to result in substantial injury and loss of life. Finally, many industries persistently violate even the lenient laws and standards they have insisted upon, and then they cover up their violations.[22]

The most serious corporate crime, however, is turning out to be the pollution of water, land, and air with toxic chemicals. Gilbert Geis, who for years has tried to shift the attention of criminologists and the public to "white-collar crime," wrote:

> The efflux from motor vehicles, plants, and incinerators of sulfur oxides, hydrocarbons, carbon monoxide, oxides of nitrogen, particulates, and many more contaminants amounts to compulsory consumption of violence by most Americans. . . . This damage, perpetuated increasingly in direct violation of local, state, and federal law, shatters people's health and safety but still escapes inclusion in the crime statistics. "Smogging" a city or town has taken on the proportions of a massive crime wave, yet federal and state statistical compilations of crime pay attention to "muggers" and ignore "smoggers."[23]

---

*In 1975 Dr. Sidney Wolfe, speaking before the House Commerce Oversight and Investigations Subcommittee, estimated that there were 3.2 million unnecessary surgeries performed each year, which resulted in 16,000 deaths; see *Washington Post*, July 16, 1975, p. A-3.

The data on white-collar crimes are not collected, categorized, tallied up in neat columns, and published in annual national reports such as the FBI's *Uniform Crime Reports*, which features frightening news about street crime. The deaths and injuries caused by law-breaking acts of respectable people—and by acts that *would* be crimes if other than powerful people committed them—are far more numerous than those caused by street crime, and many are just as gruesome. Yet the general public remains convinced that street crime is the greater threat. To a great extent, this public attitude is the creation of the mass media and opportunistic politicians. They have exaggerated its extent, decried the leniency of judges and courts toward it, and offered simplistic solutions. They have intentionally chosen to divert the attention of citizens away from other social problems, such as unemployment, inflation, the energy crisis, the proliferation of atomic weapons, war in Central America, and crime committed by so-called reputable people. The reason for the diversion is that an increase in public awareness and understanding of these other problems might lead to ameliorative policies that require some suffering or sacrifice on the part of these reputable people. Street crime, on the other hand, is a safe issue. No powerful constituency is directly damaged by a campaign against it, even a campaign that drastically escalates penalties and the number of disreputables receiving them.

If the public has been systematically deluded on the issue of crime, as I contend it has, one may still ask, what is the harm in that? Couldn't it be true, as Wilson and Kelling argue, that the symbolic benefits outweigh the harm done? In other words, though crime and disrepute are not reduced by the ineffectual efforts of the police (and in fact are probably increased by them), isn't it good that the public is made to *feel* better by seeing the police patrolling neighborhoods and "rousting" undesirables, by hearing the media report on stiff sentences delivered to persons convicted of serious crimes, by witnessing the enactment of new punitive anticrime laws (such as California's Initiative Proposition 8, the Victim's Bill of Rights, in 1982), and even by reading of the occasional execution of a murderer?

I would argue that it is not. These symbolic benefits are more than canceled out every time anger toward street crime is whipped up in support of another public policy "solution" that fails to solve anything. When nothing seems to reduce street crime and all the other distasteful and threatening forms of deviance—drug use, dereliction, prostitution, and petty property crime—a deep frustration is created in the public.

Conclusions

Reform of our jails requires either that we drastically reduce the size of the rabble class, a highly remote possibility, or that we abandon our self-serving fictions about crime and deviance. I believe that instead of arguing over which particular reform proposals might work, we should concentrate our efforts on the second task, that is, on developing and disseminating a more honest perspective on the nature and causes of crime and deviance and on the limits and consequences of various control policies. We were moving in that direction in the 1960s, and, in fact, the current intense focus on street crime is in part a reaction to the more honest (and disturbing) insights and recommendations that were developing in that period of deep societal soul-searching. In 1970 Norval Morris and Gordon Hawkins of the University of Chicago Law School published *The Honest Politician's Guide to Crime Control*, the dominant theme of which is that our delusions about crime and its control should be abandoned. The authors contend that the "overreach" of the criminal law actually "contributes to the crime problem" in several ways:

1. Where the supply of goods or services is concerned, such as narcotics, gambling, and prostitution, the criminal law operates as a "crime tariff" which makes the supply of such goods and services profitable for the criminal by driving up prices and at the same time discourages competition by those who might enter the market were it legal.

2. This leads to the development of large-scale organized criminal groups which, as in the field of legitimate business, tend to extend and diversify their operations, thus financing and promoting other criminal activity.

3. The high prices which criminal prohibition and law enforcement help to maintain have a secondary criminogenic effect in cases where demand is inelastic, as for narcotics, by causing persons to resort to crime in order to obtain the money to pay those prices.

4. The proscription of a particular form of behavior (e.g., homosexuality, prostitution, drug addiction) by the criminal law drives those who engage or participate in it into association with those engaged

in other criminal activities and leads to the growth of an extensive criminal subculture which is subversive of social order generally. It also leads, in the case of drug addiction, to endowing that pathological condition with the romantic glamour of a rebelling against authority or of some sort of elitist enterprise.

5. The expenditure of police and criminal justice resources involved in attempting to enforce statutes in relation to sexual behavior, drug taking, gambling, and other matters of private morality seriously depletes the time, energy, and manpower available for dealing with the types of crime involving violence and stealing which are the primary concern of the criminal justice system. This diversion and overextension of resources result both in failure to deal adequately with current serious crime and, because of the increased chances of impunity, in encouraging further crime.

6. These crimes lack victims, in the sense of complainants asking for the protection of the criminal law. Where such complainants are absent it is particularly difficult for the police to enforce the law. Bribery tends to flourish; political corruption of the police is invited. It is peculiarly with reference to these victimless crimes that the police are led to employ illegal means of law enforcement.

It follows therefore that any plan to deal with crime in America must first of all face this problem of the overreach of the criminal law. [It must] state clearly the nature of its priorities in regard to the use of the criminal sanction, and indicate what kinds of immoral or antisocial conduct should be removed from the current calendar of crime.[24]

Morris and Hawkins made a start. But in the fifteen years since they wrote *The Honest Politician's Guide*, we have learned more about the fallacies upon which the police and other criminal justice agencies base their actions. I believe that we are ready for an honest policy on crime control that goes beyond the criminal law and takes account of the following propositions:

1. Crime in America is not a pathological aberration of the American way, practiced only by a special category of people called criminals. It is widely and somewhat evenly spread throughout all social classes and is deeply rooted in basic American values and relationships.

2. The most serious crimes—the ones that cause great loss of money, personal injury or death, and the corruption of society's morals and political processes—are committed by reputable people.

3. Publicizing street crime committed by disreputable persons as the major crime problem in society is counterproductive in several ways:

a. It encourages crime control policies that continually fail, and this failure creates a pervasive anger and frustration in society.

b. It allows most serious crime to go unattended.

c. It may even increase street crime because the disproportionately harsh treatment given to those who commit it tends to embitter and alienate them and to perpetuate the existence of a rabble class.

While we work our way toward a more realistic and enlightened understanding of crime, we must also take care of society's day-to-day business. What should guide the right-minded public actor who must formulate policy or make decisions for the operation of the jails? The answer is simple: turn to the reasonable proposals that have been circulating among knowledgeable critics of the criminal justice system for over a decade now. Many of these recommendations were listed at the beginning of this chapter: decriminalization, diversion, expansion of pretrial release, speedy trials, humane incarceration for pretrial detainees, sentencing alternatives, and a humane system of incarceration for persons serving jail sentences. We can also begin to deal more effectively with crime and deviance and thereby indirectly influence jail policy by pursuing a new agenda:

1. We should concentrate police and penal attention on serious crime, which requires opening up the debate on what we want that term to mean.

2. In the short run, we should learn to tolerate a large number of the rabble.

3. We should work to reestablish informal, extralegal systems for controlling repulsive public deviance, particularly by taking measures that will foster a new sense of community among strangers.

4. In the long run, we should work to alter our basic values. Excessive materialism and individualism, for example, not only weaken and corrupt our personal relationships; they also help maintain a radically unequal distribution of wealth, opportunity, and prestige, which in turn produces high rates of crime and many forms of repulsive public deviance.

Progress on this agenda, if it occurs at all, will necessarily be slow. Reforming sluggish processes and static structures, particularly in the economic realm, is the work of decades, generations, even centuries. But that should not deter us, because no progress at all can be made on reforming the jail until we begin to reform our fundamental social arrangements. Until we do, the police will continue to sweep the streets of the rabble and dump them in the jails. By casting a broad net, they will snare a few disreputable persons whose crimes are serious, and these few will be punished severely. Crime rates will not be affected by these efforts; they will continue to rise and fall as they always have in response to changes in broader social arrangements. And the rabble will continue to suffer our harshest form of imprisonment, the jail—an experience that confirms their status and replenishes their ranks.

Appendix

Table A   *Race of Felony Sample*

Black	50
White	30
Mexican	5
Mexican-American	3
Cuban	3
Asian	3
El Salvadoran	2
Nicaraguan	1
Other	3

Table B   *Race of Misdemeanor Sample*

White	48
Black	42
Mexican	7
Indian	1
Filipino	1

Note: In the felony arrests we determined the race in the interviews. In the misdemeanor arrests we took the race from the booking cards, which are not as accurate, particularly in the case of Spanish-speaking persons.

Table C   *Age of Felony Sample*

18	20	22	24	26	28	30	32	34	36	38	40	42	44	46	48	50	52	54	56	58	60+
	X																				
	X																				
	X																				
	X																				
	X																				
	X		X		X																
X	X		X		X																
X	X	X	X	X	X		X														
X	X	X	X	X	X		X	X													
X	X	X	X	X	X		X	X	X												
X	X	X	X	X	X	X	X	X	X	X											
X	X	X	X	X	X	X	X	X	X	X											
X	X	X	X	X	X	X	X	X	X	X	X										
X	X	X	X	X	X	X	X	X	X	X	X	X									X
X	X	X	X	X	X	X	X	X	X	X	X	X	X								X

Table D   *Age of Misdemeanor Sample*

18	20	22	24	26	28	30	32	34	36	38	40	42	44	46	48	50	52	54	56	58	60+
	X																				
	X																				
	X					X															
	X			X		X															
	X		X	X		X															
	X		X	X		X															
	X	X	X	X	X		X	X													
	X	X	X	X	X	X	X	X	X												
	X	X	X	X	X	X	X	X	X												
	X	X	X	X	X	X	X	X	X		X										
X	X	X	X	X	X	X	X	X	X		X				X						
X	X	X	X	X	X	X	X	X	X		X		X		X	X	X		X	X	
X	X	X	X	X	X	X	X	X	X	X	X	X	X	X	X	X	X		X	X	X

Table E   *Length of Stay in Pretrial Detention of Felony Sample*

24 hours or less	40
Over 24 hours to 4 days	27
5 to 14 days	10
15 to 30 days	9
31 to 60 days	5
Over 61 days	9

Table F   *Length of Stay in Pretrial Detention of Misdemeanor Sample*

Cited and released	36
24 hours or less	50
Over 24 hours to 4 days	11
5 to 14 days	1
15 to 30 days	2

Table G   *Dispositions of Felony Sample*

Dismissed	48
Diversion	7
Fine	1
Probation	8
Fine and probation	2
Jail	18
Prison	11
Other agency	2
Failure to appear	3

Table H   *Dispositions of Misdemeanor Sample*

Dismissed	48
Diversion	2
Fine	20
Probation	2
Fine and probation	7
Jail	4
Other agency	7
Failure to appear	10

Notes

Chapter 1

1. Ronald Goldfarb, *Jails: The Ultimate Ghetto of the Criminal Justice System*, p. 29.

2. Edith Flynn, "Jails and Criminal Justice," in *Prisoners in America*, ed. Lloyd E. Ohlin, p. 57.

3. See Andrew Scull, *Decarceration*, p. 153.

4. See esp. Morton G. Wenger and Thomas A. Bonomo, "Crime, the Crisis of Capitalism, and Social Revolution," in *Crime and Capitalism*, ed. David Greenberg, pp. 420–34.

5. *Webster's Third New International Dictionary* (Springfield, Mass.: G. & C. Merriam, 1971).

6. Frances Fox Piven and Richard A. Cloward, *Regulating the Poor*, p. 7.

7. Hans Mattick, "The Contemporary Jails of the United States: An Unknown and Neglected Area of Justice," in *Handbook of Criminology*, ed. Daniel Glaser, pp. 782–83.

8. Thomas Hughes, *Alfred the Great*, pp. 181–82.

9. Ralph B. Pugh, *Imprisonment in Medieval England*, p. 3.

10. Ibid.

11. Ibid., p. 4.

12. See Henri Pirenne, *Medieval Cities*.

13. See ibid. for a description and analysis of this transition.

14. Ibid., p. 114.

15. Urban Tigner Holmes, *Daily Living in the Twelfth Century*, pp. 36–37.

16. See Douglas Hay, "Property, Authority, and the Criminal Law," in Douglas Hay et al., *Albion's Fatal Tree*.

17. Hughes, *Alfred the Great*, pp. 181–82.

18. Pugh, *Imprisonment in Medieval England*, p. 3.

19. The twenty-second act of Henry VIII (king of England, 1509–1547), quoted in William J. Chambliss, "The Law of Vagrancy," p. 73.

20. The seventh act of James I (king of England, 1603–1625) required that every county have one or more houses of correction.

21. John Howard, *The State of the Prisons*, p. 14.

22. Ronald Goldfarb notes: "By 1861, English workhouses and jails were both known simply as 'local prisons' " (*Jails*, p. 33).

23. See David Rothman, *The Discovery of the Asylum*, p. 46.

24. See ibid., ch. 1.

25. Ibid., pp. 52–56.

26. F. C. Gray, *Prison Discipline in America*, quoted in Edwin H. Sutherland and Donald R. Cressey, *Criminology*, p. 520.

27. Goldfarb, *Jails*, p. 11.

28. Walter A. Lunden, "The Rotary Jail, or Human Squirrel Cage," p. 156.

29. See ibid.

30. Kellow Chesney, *The Victorian Underworld*, p. 38.

31. James Edgar Brown, "The Increase of Crime in the United States," pp. 832–33.

32. See Chesney, *Victorian Underworld*; and Henry Mayhew, *London's Underworld*.

33. See Herbert Asbury, *The Gangs of New York City*.

34. See Troy Duster, *The Legislation of Morality*.

35. The literature on male youth gangs is large and attests to the continuity of this urban "troublemaker." For a good start, see Frederic M. Thrasher, *The Gang*.

36. See Joseph Gusfield, *The Symbolic Crusade*; and Duster, *Legislation of Morality*.

37. See Caleb Foote, "Vagrancy Type Law and Its Administration," p. 615.

38. See James Q. Wilson, *Varieties of Police Behavior*, ch. 5; and Egon Bittner, "The Police on Skid-Row: A Study of Peace Keeping."

39. Lyn Lofland, *The World of Strangers*, p. 67.

40. Personal communication from Paul Rock to Andrew Scull, quoted in Scull, *Decarceration*, p. 153.

41. See Wilson, *Varieties of Police Behavior*, ch. 5; Bittner, "Police on Skid-Row"; and Jacqueline P. Wiseman, *Stations of the Lost*, ch. 3.

42. Wiseman, *Stations of the Lost*, p. 66.

43. *San Francisco Chronicle*, March 12, 1981, p. 26.

44. Ibid., Oct. 15, 1982, p. 25.

45. Wiseman, *Stations of the Lost*, p. 67; see also Bittner, "Police on Skid-Row," for a description of this form of police work in rabble zones.

46. Bittner makes this distinction in a convincing fashion in "Police on Skid-Row."

Chapter 2

1. Marvin E. Wolfgang, Robert Figlio, and Paul Tracy, "The Seriousness of Crime: The Results of a National Survey."

2. For example, I read the following description from my interviews to two classes: A man received his weekly paycheck and noticed that he had been overpaid by $2,000. He cashed the check, went to the Tenderloin area, drank, picked up a prostitute, and went to a hotel room with her. When he woke up later, the money was gone. He assumed that she took it. He was arrested at work when he was asked to return the overpayment and indicated that he did not have it. The items that I read to the class and their scores from the center's survey (given in parentheses) were: (1) a person steals property worth $1,000 from outside a building (6.86); (2) a person cheats on his income tax return (4.49); (3) an employee embezzles $1,000 from his employer (6.22); and (4) a person knowingly passes a bad check (3.60). The average of the students' scores was 3.7.

3. This distribution of these offensive acts into the three categories—mild, moderate, and high—was made in consultation with a group of persons who have conducted research in deviance, particularly the forms of urban deviance that are common in the arrest samples.

4. For example, see Samuel E. Wallace, *Skid Row as a Way of Life*; Jacqueline P. Wiseman, *Stations of the Lost*; and James Spradley, *You Owe Yourself a Drunk*.

5. The de-institutionalization of psychiatric inmates has been described by Andrew Scull in *Decarceration*.

6. For a thorough analysis of the chaos and patterns of theft that force heroin addicts into a life of disrepute, see Marsha Rosenbaum, *Women on Heroin*, a study whose findings are valid for most male addicts as well.

7. This number seems low. San Francisco, along with New York, Chicago, Detroit, and Los Angeles, has had a large heroin problem. The samples of felony arrests in Chicago, New York, and Baltimore, referred to in the note to Table 1, have many more heroin-related arrests than my sample. Several San Francisco-based drug researchers (Dan Waldorf, Patrick Biernacki, Marsha Rosenbaum, and Shiegla Murphy) have informed me that many San Francisco heroin addicts are involved in methadone maintenance programs or are "tying over" their habits with methadone "diverted" by the program participants and

sold on the streets. Consequently many addicts are not forced into the illegal activities that render them so vulnerable to arrest.

8. Criminologists have spent a great deal of time describing—or better, romanticizing—the "thief" who observed a special thieves' code, cooperated in pulling "big scores," and possessed great criminal skills. See my own romanticizing in *The Felon*. James Incardi has done the most thorough study of this type of outlaw in *Careers in Crime*. The old-style thief is rapidly disappearing. The outlaw now coming out of the former nurturing grounds of the thief, that is, the lower-class neighborhoods, the jails, and the prisons, is a less profit-motivated and more violent and appearance-conscious individual. See my description of the new outlaw in *Prisons in Turmoil*, ch. 7.

9. See Scull, *Decarceration*.

10. A series of ethnographies over the last forty years reveals that this type persists and follows essentially the same patterns. See William Foote Whyte, *Street Corner Society*; Walter Miller, "Lower Class Culture as a Generating Milieu of Gang Delinquency"; Herbert Gans, *The Urban Villagers*; and Elliot Liebow, *Talley's Corner*.

11. The quotation is from the inscription at the base of the Statue of Liberty, written by Emma Lazarus.

12. See the appendix for the dispositions and their relationships to crime seriousness and offensiveness.

13. This relationship reverses in the case of prison sentences: 37 percent of those with medium or serious crimes and 21 percent of those with moderate or high offensiveness received prison terms.

Chapter 3

1. Hans Mattick, "The Contemporary Jails of the United States: An Unknown and Neglected Area of Justice," in *Handbook of Criminology*, ed. Daniel Glaser, p. 814.

2. See David Rothman, *The Discovery of the Asylum*.

3. Ralph B. Pugh, *Imprisonment in Medieval England*, p. 3.

4. Malcolm Feeley has recently argued that the punishment that is intentionally delivered to most persons processed by the criminal justice system is not the sentence that is imposed after conviction but the process of being held in jail before trial and having tó make court appearances; see *The Process Is the Punishment*.

5. Erving Goffman has pointed out that the individual "needs cosmetic and clothing supplies, tools for applying, arranging, and repairing them"; *Asylums*, p. 30.

6. See John Irwin, *The Felon*, ch. 5.

7. James Spradley, *You Owe Yourself a Drunk*, p. 207.

8. This does not seem to be the case in Los Angeles County where the jail operates its own laundry and cleaning enterprise. The prisoners' street clothes are cleaned and kept available for their court appearances or release.

9. Spradley, *You Owe Yourself a Drunk*, p. 207.

10. During the fall of 1980, more than half of the prisoners in my section, the mainline felony section of County Jail No. 2, requested envelopes each week and were eligible to receive them because they had less than one dollar in their property.

11. Spradley, *You Owe Yourself a Drunk*, p. 206.

12. These problems are different in other locations. For example, in Los Angeles, most of the outstanding warrants are issued by courts within the county and are routinely cleared up while the prisoner is in custody.

13. Most of the prisoners in our misdemeanor sample had their charges dismissed or were cited and released before going to court. In our felony sample, 20 percent of the prisoners had their charges dismissed before going to court, 37 percent were released on bail or OR in the first few days, and 12 percent had their charges dismissed at the first hearing. For a breakdown of the dispositions of the two samples followed in this study, see Tables G and H in the appendix.

14. Preparing for release is a major activity in prisons and mental hospitals; see Irwin, *The Felon*, ch. 4.

15. In San Francisco I heard of a few prisoners who had managed to contact persons in prisoner services or in the Northern California Service League (NCSL), a private agency. Prisoner services occasionally help a prisoner who is approaching his release day to communicate with a San Francisco County social services department where he may receive "general assistance," and NCSL supplies some clothes to released prisoners. However, only a small minority receive even these scanty aids.

Chapter 4

1. Albert Reiss, *The Police and the Public*, p. 46.

2. Jonathan Rubenstein, *City Police*, p. 274.

3. Paul Jacobs, speech delivered at a conference on prisons at Glide Memorial Church in San Francisco, autumn 1971.

4. Alan J. Davis, "Report on Sexual Assaults in the Philadelphia Prisoner System and Sheriff's Vans."

5. James Spradley, *You Owe Yourself a Drunk*, p. 162.

6. In my observation during July 1983, I saw several relatively friendly interchanges between the deputy performing the booking chores and the prisoners being booked at the Yolo County jail. The tenor of the interaction was very different from what I had observed in San Francisco and Los Angeles.

7. Alfred Schuetz, "The Stranger: An Essay in Social Psychology," described the self-disorganization a stranger experiences because of his lack of taken-for-granted preparations.

8. On a visit to the Los Angeles County jail in July 1983, I noticed a handwritten sign in the waiting room for visitors that read, "It may take eight hours for persons being bailed out to be released." The next day the sign was gone, but the deputies I questioned said that eight hours was about average.

9. *San Francisco Chronicle*, Sept. 17, 1983, p. 2.

10. *San Francisco Chronicle*, Feb. 27, 1981, p. 4.

11. At the time this was written, Gene Jimenez was a sociology graduate student who had experienced the passage into the Los Angeles County jail several times. The quotation is from his unpublished manuscript, "Cognitive Process in the Accomplishment of Stratification: Inmate Status and Roles in a Municipal Jail," p. 29.

12. Roger Martin, *Pigs and Other Animals*, pp. 59–60.

13. Jimenez, "Cognitive Process," p. 28.

14. See Leo Carroll, "Humanitarian Reform and Biracial Sexual Assault in a Maximum Security Prison."

15. These are the elements of alienation identified and analyzed by Melvin Seeman in his classic review of the concept as it has appeared in the literature: "On the Meaning of Alienation."

16. Erich Fromm, *The Sane Society*, p. 124.

17. Gwynn Nettler, "A Measure of Alienation," p. 672.

18. Emile Durkheim, *Suicide*, ch. 5.

19. Schuetz, "The Stranger."

20. Irwin, *The Felon*, p. 117.

Chapter 5

1. See *Los Angeles Times*, Dec. 14, 1983, pt. 1, p. 2, and Dec. 15, 1983, pt. 1, pp. 3, 17; and *People Weekly*, Feb. 13, 1984, pp. 30–31.

2. Erving Goffman, *Asylums*, p. 43.

3. Goffman, "On the Characteristics of Total Institutions," in ibid.

4. Most of these have been recognized and analyzed by Goffman, in ibid.

5. One of Goffman's major contributions to sociology is his convincing analysis of how persons "present" themselves through behavior and how important this presentation is in their definitions of self. See his *Presentation of Self in Everyday Life*.

6. Goffman, *Asylums*, p. 20.

7. Usually when prisoners have or develop a serious medical problem, they are transferred to a hospital. Both Los Angeles and San Francisco General Hospitals have special wards for jail prisoners. There are occasions, however,

when prisoners cannot convince the jail's staff that they do have serious problems, and so they go untreated.

8. In a survey of 2,452 of the nation's jails conducted by the National Sheriffs' Association, the respondents indicated that a medical doctor worked at the jail for an average of 3.9 hours a day, a nurse 9.8 hours a day, and a physician's assistant 9.7 hours a day. See National Sheriffs' Association, *The State of the Nation's Jails*, p. 207.

9. The respondents to the National Sheriffs' Association survey indicated that on the average, jail prisoners spend 6.3 hours a week in "outdoor recreation." Ibid., p. 213.

10. The police were first introduced in London as a response to the rabble, who were then spoken of as "the dangerous classes." See Alan Silver, "The Demand for Order in Civil Society," in *The Police*, ed. David Bordua.

11. Many similar verbal attacks on the deputies occurred while I was observing in the booking room. If the prisoner persisted, he was firmly warned, and if he still persisted, the deputies roughly removed him to an isolation cell. In the Los Angeles County jail such outbursts were not tolerated; they precipitated either a severe warning or instant removal to an isolation cell.

12. Roger Martin, *Pigs and Other Animals*, p. 57. Personal observation has persuaded me that the vast majority of prisoner requests are motivated by nothing more than a desire to improve upon reduced circumstances. Martin's conclusion that prisoners intended to take advantage of him made it easier for him to turn down their requests and accept the collective cynicism.

13. Ibid., pp. 54, 75.

14. Ibid., p. 149.

15. Malcolm Feeley, *The Process Is the Punishment*, p. 15.

16. For a vivid description of the use of judicial spectacle and ceremony in earlier English courts, see Douglas Hay, "Property, Authority, and the Criminal Law," in Douglas Hay et al., *Albion's Fatal Tree*, p. 27.

17. Letter from John Hersey dated Aug. 11, 1972, quoted in Feeley, *Process Is the Punishment*, pp. 8–9.

18. Anthony G. Amsterdam, "The Supreme Court and the Rights of Suspects: Criminal Cases," p. 408.

19. Quoted in David Greenberg, "Donald Black's So-Called Theory of Law," p. 6.

20. This is Malcolm Feeley's important thesis: the primary purpose of the court process is not to determine legal guilt through due process or, as many critics have argued, to run an efficient system through plea bargaining, but rather to punish most defendants through the court process. He suggests that the sanctioning powers are distributed among several people—the arresting officers, bail bondsmen, defense attorneys, prosecutors, and judges—and that punishment is contained in the arrest, jail experience, and court appearances;

see *Process Is the Punishment*, pp. 31–32. In the samples I followed in my research, slightly less than half of the felony charges and more than 50 percent of the misdemeanor charges were dismissed. Another 18 percent of those arrested for a felony and more than 31 percent of those arrested for a misdemeanor were diverted, fined, or granted probation without jail sentences. The vast majority of misdemeanor charges were dismissed or otherwise disposed of within forty-eight hours of arrest, and half of the persons arrested for a felony were released from jail within seventy-two hours. However, the process of arrest, booking, and being jailed is extremely punitive. Moreover, some categories of people were held longer before having their cases dismissed or disposed of through diversion or probation. Thirteen of the petty hustlers (46 percent) had their cases dismissed, but they waited an average of 5.3 days to be released. Among the rabble or marginal rabble types forty-two out of the 100 arrested for a felony had their cases dismissed, but eleven of them were held for more than three days, and four were held more than fifteen days. In some other counties, persons are held much longer before dismissal. In a "tracking sample" of 2,255 persons arrested for misdemeanors and felonies in San Mateo County from November 1981 to October 1982, the eighty-two persons who had their cases dismissed by the court or the district attorney had remained in jail for an average of thirteen days; see Institute for Law and Police Planning, *San Mateo County Needs Assessment* (Oakland, Ca., 1983). In Miami in 1981 and 1982, over 66 percent of all felony charges were dismissed, and those who waited in jail for dismissal spent an average of fifty days there; the median stay was twenty-one days; see James Austin, Barry Krisberg, and Paul Litsky, *Supervised Pretrial Release Test Design Evaluation*.

Chapter 6

1. In *Becoming Deviant*, David Matza suggests that appreciation requires a suspension of moral judgment and an interest in understanding the deviant individual rather than in avoiding him. In jail, avoidance is impossible, and a certain amount of understanding is therefore essential.

2. The discovery of these outsider viewpoints was an important development in the sociology of deviance and has been reviewed and analyzed many times. See esp. ibid.

3. Jacqueline Wiseman, *Stations of the Lost*, p. 16.

4. See my earlier attempt to describe some of these views in *The Felon*, ch. 1.

5. Gerald Suttles, *The Social Order of the Slum*, pp. 4–9.

6. James Spradley, *You Owe Yourself a Drunk*, p. 20.

7. Students of deviant behavior, who developed "deviant subculture" as one of their major explanatory concepts, have not followed the suggestion of J. Milton Yinger in his early essay "Contraculture and Subculture." Influ-

enced by Albert Cohen's argument that delinquent boys were reacting to mid-dle-class values in their development of delinquent patterns, Yinger suggested that we recognize a special deviant cultural system—a "contraculture" that "raises to a position of prominence one particular kind of dynamic linkage between norms and personality: the creation of a series of inverse or counter values [opposed to those of the surrounding society]" (p. 628). Instead, soci-ologists studying deviant behavior treated the society as a vast conglomeration of subcultures, many of them more or less deviant; they postulated a situation of pluralism rather than of opposition. Conflict sociologists introduced the idea that some deviant subcultures are incipient revolutionary forms; but this is not the same thing. Cohen's delinquent boys were not revolutionaries but simply boys reacting toward middle-class institutions and values by turning conventional patterns upside down. Whether or not this is a useful way of un-derstanding delinquent behavior in the 1950s, I believe the idea of opposition is becoming more relevant. In recent years, opposition values, which are more nihilistic than revolutionary, are taking shape, and they seem to be circulating mostly among the "deviants" who occupy the rabble category. See Albert Cohen, *Delinquent Boys*.

8. David B. Rottman, "The Social Context of Jails."

9. Spradley, *You Owe Yourself a Drunk*, p. 204.

10. Most jails allow paperbacks to circulate but have no adequate system for obtaining or distributing them. Of the jail administrators responding to the National Sheriffs' Association survey (*The State of the Nation's Jails*), 25 per-cent said they had a library. Many jails have ties with public libraries, but the selection of books is usually limited and the distribution of books sluggish and irregular. Prisoners with money or friends outside often purchase or receive magazines and newspapers, and these circulate in the tanks until they disinte-grate.

11. Rottman, "Social Context of Jails," p. 11.

12. Malcolm Braly, *False Starts*, pp. 125–26.

13. Edwin Sutherland and Donald R. Cressey, *Criminology*, ch. 4.

14. Wiseman, *Stations of the Lost*, p. 38.

15. Ibid., p. 44.

16. Braly, *False Starts*, p. 126.

17. See Marvin E. Wolfgang, Terence P. Thornberry, and Robert M. Fi-glio, *From Boy to Man: From Delinquency to Crime*.

18. Jack Abbott, *In the Belly of the Beast*, p. 13.

Chapter 7

1. Hans Mattick, "The Contemporary Jails of the United States: An Un-known and Neglected Area of Justice," in *Handbook of Criminology*, ed. Dan-iel Glaser, p. 822.

2. Edith Flynn, "Jails and Criminal Justice," in *Prisoners in America*, ed. Lloyd E. Ohlin, p. 76.

3. Ronald Goldfarb, *Jails: The Ultimate Ghetto of the Criminal Justice System*, p. 453.

4. National Advisory Commission on Criminal Justice Standards and Goals, *Report on Corrections*, p. 133.

5. Goldfarb, *Jails*, p. 450.

6. Besides the proposals by Mattick, Flynn, and Goldfarb quoted above, and others like them, sets of standards have been developed by many individuals and government bodies, notably Myrl E. Alexander, in *Jail Administration*, and the National Advisory Commission on Criminal Justice Standards and Goals, *Report on Corrections*. The most recent and perhaps the most complete set of standards is contained in *The Little Red Jail Book*, prepared for the American Friends Service Committee by its Criminal Justice Committee in 1983. In the 1970s intense interest in jail reform led to the establishment in Boulder, Colorado, of the Jail Center, a branch of the National Institute of Corrections, which has attempted to improve American jails through a variety of research and training programs. For examples of two successfully implemented reforms, see the descriptions of the Benton County jail in Oregon and the Hampton County jail in Massachusetts, in Mark Pogerebin, *Managing Scarce Resources for Jails: Information Package*. This report was produced by a grant processed through the Jail Center.

7. Goldfarb, *Jails*, p. 448.

8. For a thorough examination of this status, see David Matza, "Position and Behavior Patterns of Youth," in *Handbook of Modern Sociology*, ed. Robert E. Faris, pp. 191–216.

9. For an analysis of the relative permanence of the "absolute poor" and their relationship to the rabble class, see David Matza and Henry Miller, "Poverty and Proletariat," in *Contemporary Social Problems*, ed. Robert K. Merton and Robert Nisbet, pp. 639–73.

10. Charles Loring Brace, *The Dangerous Classes of New York and Twenty Years' Work Among Them*, p. 29.

11. Svend Ranulf, *Moral Indignation and Middle-Class Psychology*, esp. pp. 41–46.

12. Erving Goffman, *Relations in Public*, p. 329.

13. See esp. James Q. Wilson, *Thinking About Crime*, ch. 5.

14. Wilson's book, *Thinking About Crime*, and his articles in the *Atlantic Monthly, Commentary, The Public Interest*, and the *New York Times Sunday Magazine* have been widely read.

15. James Q. Wilson and George Kelling, "Broken Windows," pp. 29–30.

16. Ibid., p. 31.

17. *Los Angeles Times*, Aug. 27, 1982, pt. 1, pp. 1, 3.

18. Joseph Wambaugh, *The Glitter Dome*, pp. 56–57.

19. *Los Angeles Times*, Aug. 21, 1982, pt. 2, p. 1.

20. Ibid., pp. 1, 6.

21. Marshal B. Clinard and Peter G. Yeager, *Corporate Crime*, p. 8.

22. See Joseph Page and Mary Win O'Brien, *Bitter Wages*; Rachel Scott, *Muscle and Blood*; and Paul Brodeur, *Expendable Americans*.

23. Gilbert Geis, "Deterring Corporate Crime," in *Corporate Power in America*, ed. Ralph Nader and Mark J. Green, p. 12.

24. Norval Morris and Gordon Hawkins, *The Honest Politician's Guide to Crime Control*, pp. 5–6.

Bibliography

Abbott, Jack. *In the Belly of the Beast*. New York: Random House, 1981.

Alexander, Myrl E. *Jail Administration*. Springfield, Ill.: C. Thomas, 1957.

American Friends Service Committee. *Struggle for Justice*. New York: Hill & Wang, 1971.

————. *The Little Red Jail Book*. San Francisco: Criminal Justice Committee, Northern California Regional Office, 1983.

Amsterdam, Anthony G. "The Supreme Court and the Rights of Suspects: Criminal Cases." In *The Rights of Americans*. Edited by Norman Dorsen, pp. 401–32. New York: Random House, 1970.

Asbury, Herbert. *The Gangs of New York City*. New York: Capricorn Books, 1927.

Austin, James, Barry Krisberg, and Paul Litsky. *Supervised Pretrial Release Test Design Evaluation*. San Francisco: National Council on Crime and Delinquency, 1983.

Bittner, Egon. "The Police on Skid-Row: A Study of Peace Keeping." *American Sociological Review* 32 (Oct. 1967): 699–715.

Brace, Charles Loring. *The Dangerous Classes of New York and Twenty Year's Work Among Them*. New York: Wynkoop & Hallenbeck, 1880.

Braly, Malcolm. *False Starts*. Middlesex, England: Penguin Books, 1976.

Brodeur, Paul. *Expendable Americans*. New York: Viking Press, 1974.

Brown, James Edgar. "The Increase of Crime in the United States." *The Independent*, April 1970, pp. 832–33.

Carroll, Leo. "Humanitarian Reform and Biracial Sexual Assault in a Maximum Security Prison." *Urban Life* 6 (Jan. 1977): 417–37.

Chambliss, William J. "The Law of Vagrancy." *Social Problems* 12 (1964): 67–77.

Chesney, Kellow. *The Victorian Underworld*. New York: Schocken Books, 1972.

Clinard, Marshal B., and Peter G. Yeager. *Corporate Crime*. New York: Free Press, 1980.

Cohen, Albert. *Delinquent Boys*. New York: Free Press, 1955.

Davis, Alan J. "Report on Sexual Assaults in the Philadelphia Prisoner System and Sheriff's Vans." Distributed by the Pennsylvania Prison Society, Philadelphia, Pa., 1968.

Durkheim, Emile. *Suicide*. New York: Free Press, 1951.

Duster, Troy. *The Legislation of Morality*. New York: Free Press, 1970.

————. "Social Implications of the 'New' Black Urban Underclass." Unpublished paper on file at the Institute for the Study of Social Change, University of California, Berkeley, 1984.

Eisenstein, James, and Herbert Jacob. *Felony Justice*. Boston: Little, Brown, 1977.

Feeley, Malcolm. *The Process Is the Punishment*. New York: Russell Sage, 1979.

Flynn, Edith. "Jails and Criminal Justice." In *Prisoners in America*. Edited by Lloyd E. Ohlin, pp. 49–85. Englewood Cliffs, N.J.: Prentice-Hall, 1973.

Foote, Caleb. "Vagrancy Type Law and Its Administration." *University of Pennsylvania Law Review* 104 (1956): 603–50.

Freed, Daniel J., and Patricia M. Wald. *Bail in the United States*. Washington, D.C.: U.S. Department of Justice; New York: Vera Foundation, 1964.

Fromm, Erich. *The Sane Society*. New York: Rinehart, 1955.

Gans, Herbert. *The Urban Villagers*. New York: Free Press, 1962.

Geis, Gilbert. "Deterring Corporate Crime." In *Corporate Power in America*. Edited by Ralph Nader and Mark J. Green, pp. 182–97. New York: Grossman, 1973.

Goffman, Erving. *Presentation of Self in Everyday Life*. New York: Doubleday, 1959.

————. *Asylums*. Garden City, N.Y.: Anchor Books, 1961.

————. *Relations in Public*. New York: Harper & Row, 1971.

Goldfarb, Ronald. *Jails: The Ultimate Ghetto of the Criminal Justice System*. New York: Doubleday, 1975.

Greenberg, David. "Donald Black's So-Called Theory of Law." Unpublished paper presented to the Conference on Critical Legal Studies, Minneapolis, 1980.

Gusfield, Joseph. *The Symbolic Crusade*. Urbana: University of Illinois Press, 1963.

Hay, Douglas. "Property, Authority, and the Criminal Law." In Douglas Hay et al., *Albion's Fatal Tree*. New York: Pantheon Books, 1975, pp. 17–63.

Holmes, Urban Tigner. *Daily Living in the Twelfth Century*. Madison: University of Wisconsin Press, 1952.

Howard, John. *The State of the Prisons in England and Wales*. 2d ed. London: Cadell and Conant, 1780.

Hughes, Thomas. *Alfred the Great*. London: Macmillan, 1881.

Incardi, James. *Careers in Crime*. Chicago: Rand-McNally, 1975.

Institute for Law and Police Planning. *San Mateo County Needs Assessment*. Oakland, Ca., 1983.

Irwin, John. *The Felon*. Englewood Cliffs, N.J.: Prentice-Hall, 1970.

———. *Prisons in Turmoil*. Boston: Little, Brown, 1980.

Jimenez, Gene. "Cognitive Process in the Accomplishment of Stratification: Inmate Status and Roles in a Municipal Jail." Unpublished manuscript, 1975.

Kaplan, John, and Jerome Skolnick. *Criminal Justice*. Mineola, N.Y.: Foundation Press, 1982.

Liebow, Elliot. *Talley's Corner*. Boston: Little, Brown, 1967.

Lofland, Lyn. *The World of Strangers*. New York: Basic Books, 1973.

Lunden, Walter A. "The Rotary Jail, or Human Squirrel Cage." *Journal of the Society of Architectural Historians* 18(4) (1959): 149–57.

Martin, Roger. *Pigs and Other Animals*. Arcadia, Ca.: Myco Publishing House, 1980.

Mattick, Hans. "The Contemporary Jails of the United States: An Unknown and Neglected Area of Justice." In *Handbook of Criminology*. Edited by Daniel Glaser, pp. 777–848. Chicago: Rand-McNally, 1974.

Matza, David. "Position and Behavior Patterns of Youth." In *Handbook of Modern Sociology*. Edited by Robert E. Faris, pp. 191–216. Chicago: Rand-McNally, 1964.

———. *Becoming Deviant*. Englewood Cliffs, N.J.: Prentice-Hall, 1969.

Matza, David, and Henry Miller. "Poverty and Proletariat." In *Contemporary Social Problems*. 4th ed. Edited by Robert K. Merton and Robert Nisbet, pp. 639–73. New York: Harcourt Brace Jovanovich, 1976.

Mayhew, Henry. *London's Underworld*. Selections from vol. 4 of *London Labour and the London Poor*. Edited by Peter Quennell. London: W. Kimber, 1950.

Miller, Walter. "Lower-Class Culture as a Generating Milieu of Gang Delinquency." *Journal of Social Issues* 14 (1958): 5–19.

Moynahan, J. M., and Earle K. Stewart. *The American Jail*. Chicago: Nelson-Hall, 1980.

Morris, Norval, and Gordon Hawkins. *The Honest Politician's Guide to Crime Control*. Chicago: University of Chicago Press, 1970.

National Advisory Commission on Criminal Justice Standards and Goals. *Report on Corrections*. Washington, D.C., 1973.

National Sheriffs' Association. *The State of the Nation's Jails*. N.p., 1982.

Nettler, Gwynn. "A Measure of Alienation." *American Sociological Review* 22 (1957): 670–77.

Packer, Herbert. *The Limits of the Criminal Sanction*. Palo Alto, Ca.: Stanford University Press, 1968.

Page, Joseph, and Mary Win O'Brien. *Bitter Wages*. New York: Grossman, 1973.

Pirenne, Henri. *Medieval Cities*. Translated from the French by Frank D. Halsey. Princeton: Princeton University Press, 1969.

Piven, Frances Fox, and Richard A. Cloward. *Regulating the Poor*. New York: Pantheon Books, 1971.

Pogerebin, Mark. *Managing Scarce Resources for Jails: Information Package*. Unpublished report to the National Institute of Corrections, Washington, D.C., 1981.

Pugh, Ralph B. *Imprisonment in Medieval England*. Cambridge, England: Cambridge University Press, 1968.

Queen, Stuart A. *The Passing of the County Jail*. Menasha, Wis.: Banta, 1920.

Ranulf, Svend. *Moral Indignation and Middle-Class Psychology*. Copenhagen: Levin & Munksgaard, 1938.

Reiss, Albert. *The Police and the Public*. New Haven: Yale University Press, 1972.

Robinson, Louis N. *Jails: Care and Treatment of Misdemeanant Prisoners in the United States*. New York: Winston, 1944.

Rohrlich, Ted. "Jail Inmate Dies While Rules Hold Guard 'Prisoner.'" *Los Angeles Times*, April 30, 1983, part 2, pp. 1, 8.

Rosenbaum, Marsha. *Women on Heroin*. New Brunswick, N.J.: Rutgers University Press, 1981.

Rothman, David. *The Discovery of the Asylum*. Boston: Little, Brown, 1971.

Rottman, David B. "The Social Context of Jails." Paper presented at the 1974 Annual Meeting of the American Sociological Association, Montreal, 1974.

Rubenstein, Jonathan. *City Police*. New York: Farrar, Straus & Giroux, 1973.

Schuetz, Alfred. "The Stranger: An Essay in Social Psychology." *American Journal of Sociology* 49 (1944): 499–507.

Scott, Rachel. *Muscle and Blood*. New York: E. P. Dutton, 1974.

Scull, Andrew. *Decarceration*. Englewood Cliffs, N.J.: Prentice-Hall, 1977.

Seeman, Melvin. "On the Meaning of Alienation." *American Sociological Review* 24 (1959): 783–91.

Silver, Alan. "The Demand for Order in Civil Society." In *The Police*. Edited by David Bordua, pp. 1–24. New York: John Wiley & Sons, 1967.

Spradley, James. *You Owe Yourself a Drunk*. Boston: Little, Brown, 1970.

Sutherland, Edwin H., and Donald R. Cressey. *Criminology*. 10th ed. New York: J. P. Lippincott, 1978.

Suttles, Gerald. *The Social Order of the Slum*. Chicago: University of Chicago Press, 1968.

Thrasher, Frederic M. *The Gang*. Chicago: University of Chicago Press, 1936.

U.S. Department of Justice. *Source Book of Criminal Justice Statistics*. Washington, D.C.: Bureau of Justice Statistics, 1981.

Vera Institute of Justice. *Felony Arrests: Their Prosecution and Disposition in New York City's Courts*. New York, 1977.

Wallace, Samuel E. *Skid Row as a Way of Life*. Totowa, N.J.: Bedminster Press, 1965.

Wambaugh, Joseph. *The Glitter Dome*. New York: Bantam Books, 1981.

Wenger, Morton G., and Thomas A. Bonomo. "Crime, the Crisis of Capitalism, and Social Revolution." In *Crime and Capitalism*. Edited by David Greenberg, pp. 420–34. Palo Alto, Ca.: Mayfield, 1981.

Whyte, William Foote. *Street Corner Society*. Chicago: University of Chicago Press, 1943.

Wilson, James Q. *Varieties of Police Behavior*. Cambridge, Mass.: Harvard University Press, 1968.

———. *Thinking About Crime*. New York: Random House, 1975.

Wilson, James Q., and George Kelling. "Broken Windows." *Atlantic Monthly*, March 1982, pp. 29–38.

Wiseman, Jacqueline P. *Stations of the Lost*. Englewood Cliffs, N.J.: Prentice-Hall, 1970.

Wolfgang, Marvin E., Robert Figlio, and Paul Tracy. "The Seriousness of Crime: The Results of a National Survey." Final report to the Bureau of Justice Statistics, Washington, D.C., 1981.

Wolfgang, Marvin E., Terence P. Thornberry, and Robert M. Figlio. *From Boy to Man: From Delinquency to Crime*. Chicago: University of Chicago Press, 1985.

Yinger, J. Milton. "Contraculture and Subculture." *American Sociological Review* 25 (Oct. 1960): 625–35.

Index

Abbot, Jack, as example of outlaw type, 99–100

Acts of Settlement (England), 10

Age: at first arrest, and subsequent criminal activity, 99; of persons in felony and misdemeanor samples, 120 (tables); as prejudicial factor in campaign against rabble, 107; problems of, facing American youth, 103–4

Alameda County, California, jail experiences in, 89

Alcoholism: criminalization of, 9, 10; and derelicts in rabble population, 9, 27–28; and diversion for alcohol-related offenses, 101. *See also* Drunkenness, arrests for

Alfred the Great, 3, 5

Alienation, and condition of jailed persons, 64

Aliens, 40, 63; in felony arrest sample, 34–36, 39. *See also individual nationalities by name*

American Friends Service Committee, on misuse of discretionary power, 102n

Amsterdam, Anthony, on antiprisoner attitudes of judges, 81–82

Anomie, and condition of jailed persons, 64, 65

Arrests: analysis of, 18–41; degrading aspects of, 67–68; differences in experiences during, 61–63; and discretionary standards, 11, 16, 28; distributions of felony and misdemeanor samples of, 39; felony, by city, 19; loss of freedom of choice in, 54; offensiveness and, 23–25; punitive aspects of, 130n.20; for purposes of controlling rabble population, 15; and seriousness of crime, 19–23; shock of, as cause of disorientation, 53–56; and types of disreputables, 25–39

Asians, in felony sample, 119 (table)

Asylums, used to manage problem populations, 7

Atascadero, California, institute for criminally insane in, 31

Attachment, as jail substitute, 5

Attitudinal degradation, 73–78; by police, 74–75; by sheriffs' deputies, 75–78

Attorneys: attitudes of, toward prisoners, 81–83; clothing styles of, 79n

Authority: police establishment of, 54–55; and techniques used by police in arrests, 55

Bailey, F. Lee, arrest of, 68n

Bail system, 42–43; in England, 5–6; proposals for abolition of, 102

Baltimore, Maryland, distribution of felony arrests in, 19

Benton County jail, Oregon, 132n.6

Biernacki, Patrick, drug-use research of, 125n.7

Bittner, Egon, 16
Black Death, 6n
Blacks: examples of police treatment of, 108–9; in felony and misdemeanor samples, 119 (tables); youth unemployment among, 104n
Booking process: attitude of booking officers toward prisoners in, 57–58; as cause of disorientation, 56–59; degrading conditions during, 57; punitive aspect of, 130n.20
Boulder, Colorado, Jail Center in, 132n.6
Brace, Charles Loring, on threat to society from "dangerous classes," 105
Bracton, Henry de, on punishment in English jails, 44
Braly, Malcolm, on learning criminal patterns in jails, 95
Bridewells (English workhouses), 6
Business, personal, ability to deal with: as component of social stability, 46–47; loss of, by prisoners, 51–52

California: "lowrider" culture in, 9 (see also Lowriders); punitive anticriminal laws in, 114
California Guidance Center (Vacaville), 31
California Rehabilitation Center (Norco), 29
Center for Studies in Criminology and Criminal Law (University of Pennsylvania), 20
Central Americans, as focus of police scrutiny, 35
Chesney, Kellow, on "dangerous classes," 8–9
Chicago, Illinois, distribution of felony arrests in, 19
"Cholos," 9, 39n
"Citation" programs, for misdemeanor offenses, 42–43
Civil War: development of rabble class after, 9; jail system in time of, 8
Clinard, Marshal, on cost of corporate crime, 112
Cloward, Richard, on social control of the poor, 2–3
Cohen, Albert, on delinquency as response to middle-class values, 131n.7
Commitment to society, loss of, as part of degradation process, 83–84

Containment of rabble, 11–13
Contested zones, stringent police standards in, 13
Corner boys: in felony arrest sample, 31–33, 39; jail experience of, 63; role of, in jail hierarchy, 94
Court system: attitude toward prisoners in, 78–83; Feeley's thesis on goal of, 129–30n.20. See also Attorneys; Bail system; Judicial system
Crazies, in felony arrest sample, 30–31, 39, 40
Crime: and punitive anticrime laws, 114; street and "reputable," compared, 112–15, 116; victimless, and diversion of resources, 116. See also Street crime
Crime causation: and acculturation process in jails, 96–97; criminal law as factor in, 115–16
Crime Control Model of criminal justice (Packer), 73
Crime seriousness: and arrests, 19–23; difference between offensiveness and, 23–24; and offensiveness, 23–25, 25 (table), 40–41, 40 (table); ranking of, 21, 125nn.2, 3; survey of, 20, 22
Criminalization of drugs and alcohol, and control of deviant population, 9, 10
Criminal justice officials: degradation of prisoners by, 67; misuse of discretionary power by, 102n; punishment of rabble by, 102–3, 126n.4, 129–30n.20
Criminal law, proposals for reform of, 116–18
Crusades, 4
Cubans: in felony sample, 119 (table); as focus of police scrutiny, 35–36
Cultural preparation, for rabble life, 91–97

"Dangerous classes," definition and categories of, 8–9, 105. See also Disreputables; Rabble
Decriminalization, proposals for, 101, 117
Defiance, as characteristic of rabble mentality, 90–91
Degradation, 67–84; attitudinal, 73–78; judicial, 78–83; and loss of commitment, 83–84; and loss of identity, 70–71; and personal hygiene considera-

London, England, origin of police in, 129n.10

Los Angeles, California: "cholos" in, 9; experience of young black males in, 110–11. *See also* Los Angeles County Jail

Los Angeles County Jail, 44; booking procedure in, 58–59; improvisation in, 90; judicial restraints imposed on deputies in, 77–78; and length of time required for bailing out, 128n.8; medical screening in, 72, 128n.7 (ch. 5); and shock of jail experience, 63; study of, xii; tank layout in, 59; types of disreputable arrestees in, 39n; and wariness toward deputies, 90

Lowriders, 9; characteristics of, 33–34; in felony arrest sample, 33–34, 39; in jail hierarchy, 94; and origin of term, 33

Making do, as characteristic of rabble mentality, 89–90

Martin, Roger: on attitudes of deputies toward prisoners, 76–77; on experience of square johns in jail, 62

Mattick, Hans: decriminalization proposals of, 101; on historical predecessors of jail, 3; on jail security, 44

Matza, David, on need to understand deviant individuals in jail, 130n.1

Medical services provided to jailed prisoners, 71–72, 128–29nn.7, 8

Mental hospitals, and released patients among arrest sample, 27, 30–31

Methadone maintenance programs, 125–26n.7

Mexican-Americans, in felony sample, 119 (table)

Mexicans: in felony and misdemeanor samples, 119 (tables); as target of police scrutiny, 35, 37

Miami, Florida, disposition of felony charges in, 130n.20

Minority status, as characteristic of jail population, 2

Misdemeanors, arrests for, 18, 39; age of persons in sample of, 120 (table); "citation" program for, 42–43; disposition of, 121 (table), 127n.13, 130n.20; distribution of, 20 (table); and length of stay in pretrial detention, 121 (ta-

ble); race of persons in sample of, 119 (table); types of persons involved in, 39

Moon, Sun Yung, 38

Moral enterprise, law viewed as, and degradation of prisoners, 83–84

Morris, Norval, analysis of crime by, 115–16

Murder, by reputable persons, 112–13

Murphy, Shiegla, drug-use research by, 125n.7

Narcotic law violations. *See* Drug use, narcotic

Nettler, Gwynn, and use of alienation concept, 64–65

Newark, New Jersey, study of police tactics in, 107

Newgate jail (New York City), 7

New Haven, Connecticut, court system in, 78

New Orleans, Louisiana, Goldfarb's proposed jail reform in, 103

New York: distribution of felony arrests in, 19; early jails in, 7; gangs in, 9

Nicaraguans, in felony sample, 119 (table)

Normlessness, 65

Offensiveness: and arrests, 23–25; defined, 23; differentiated from crime seriousness, 23–24; ranking of, 24, 125nn.2, 3; relationship of, to crime seriousness, 24–25, 25 (table), 40 (table), 40–41; as trigger to arrest, 40

Opiate addiction, 9

Opportunism, as characteristic of rabble mentality, 88–89

OR. *See* Own recognizance release

Orange County jail, California, 62

Outlaws: in felony arrest sample, 29–30, 39, 40; in medieval times, 29–30; as prison hero, 91; studies on, 126n.8

Own recognizance (OR) release, xii, 42, 101–2

Packer, Herbert L., on models of criminal justice system, 73

"Peace-keeping" police activity, rabble control by, 10

Petty crime: campaign against, as diversion, 111–12; and role of petty crimi-

Wariness, as characteristic of rabble mentality, 87–88
"Watchman" style of police rabble management, 10
White-collar crime, cost and seriousness of, 112–14
Whites, in felony and misdemeanor samples, 119 (tables)
Wilson, James Q., on campaign against rabble, 107, 109, 111, 114
Wiseman, Jacqueline: on mentality of Skid Row types, 87; on rabble management, 15; on social life of disreputables, 97
Wolfe, Sidney, Dr., on deaths attributable to unnecessary surgeries, 113n
Wolfgang, Marvin: study of arrests by,

99; survey of crime severity by, 20, 22
Women, not included in study, xiii
Workhouses, in England, 6

Yeager, Peter, on cost of corporate crime, 112
Yinger, J. Milton, on deviant cultural system, 130–31n.7
Yolo County, California, xii; booking procedures in jail in, 59; and humanitarian attitude toward prisoners, 78, 127n.6; jail facilities of, 44n, 59; and types of disreputables, 39n
Youths: literature on, 124n.35; problems faced by, and rabble existence, 103–4. *See also* Delinquency

Compositor: Wilsted & Taylor
Text: Times Roman
Display: Goudy Bold & Times Roman
Printer: Vail-Ballou Press
Binder: Vail-Ballou Press